The Great
EXCHANGE

PASSING THE BATON BETWEEN
GENERATIONS OF WORLD SHAPERS

TERRY R. BONE

ISBN 978-0-9783947-5-2

I dedicate this book to our
grandchildren beginning with
Abigail Kaelin Gray.

Abby, you are the forerunner for an
unstoppable generation.

All this I have in writing from the hand of the Lord upon me.
And He gave me understanding in all the details.

1 Chron. 28:19

FOREWORD

Several years ago, I had a vision during a personal time of prayer.

I saw the running track at our local High School surrounded by bleachers filled with people. There were thousands of people milling about at concession stands and excitedly buzzing in their seats as they waited for the race to begin. The atmosphere was charged with anticipation - it felt like an Olympic event was about to start.

Suddenly, I was down on the track. The participants in the upcoming race were stretching and preparing to run in what was clearly a relay race. I recognized many faces of pastors and ministry colleagues. There were many other faces of people I do not know. The runners taking the first leg of the relay were men, my Dad's age in their 60's. The second leg were runners around my age, late 30's, and after them were runners in their 20's. I sensed there were more runners, but I could not see them yet.

The scene changed quickly. The race began and fans were cheering wild and loud as the first runners made their way around the track. As the first lap neared its end and the baton was about to be passed, my vantage point changed yet again.

I had a cinematic close-up on the face of one of the older runners. His teammate was ready to take the baton and sprint off into the next lap. But this man glanced down at the baton and then over at the stands filled with cheering, adoring fans. *In that moment a look of decision came over the runner's face as he tucked the baton firmly next to his side and strode past his waiting teammate.*

In my vision, this same unorthodox event happened in every lane on the track. Runners decided to keep running with their batons for yet another lap.

I could see the confusion on the faces of the fans. The fever pitch of excitement toned down a bit. But then, as the runners came round again to the transition point, the anticipation mounted again. Finally, the baton would pass, and the race would continue according to plan. But it didn't happen. *Once again, the baton was not passed.*

Confusion increased in the stands and on the field as, lap after lap, the older generation continued running past their ready and willing counterparts. I saw the fans quiet down and ultimately pack up and leave. I saw the awaiting runners sit down, put their track suits back on, grab their backpacks and leave. The field and the stands emptied out with the exception of a couple of disillusioned runners about my age; standing and looking and waiting.

The big outdoor lights that are used to illuminate nighttime sporting events came on. The bleachers were empty. Empty popcorn boxes and trampled soft drink cups blew across the running track like dusty tumbleweed from an old western movie.

The older generation who had been running for what seemed like hours were now exhausted. As they each slowly made their way around the track, they looked up and saw no one was watching anymore. The stands were empty. It wasn't fun anymore. They were done. They staggered toward their respective transition points, covered in sweat, beleaguered and worn out.

I saw a close up of the first runner's face whom I had previously seen at the beginning of the race. He had a look of disgust on his face, as there was no one waiting to take the baton from him. In my vision, it was as though I could hear his internal thought process: *"What is wrong with this next generation? Where are they?"*

With no one there to continue, the runners all dropped their batons on the ground. Their personal 'victory' became a corporate defeat. No runners left. No relay completed. No one interested in the stands. No energy. No joy. Then my vision was over.

When Pastors and leaders fail to pass the baton of ministry, next generation runners lose heart and leave the track of ministry. The cloud of witnesses in the bleachers become confused as the race no longer makes sense. The whole intent of the baton of ministry is lost, and there are no winners. Anywhere.

We cannot hold onto the batons of ministry as though the baton is the trophy itself. The trophy is won after this life. We must run well and transition to the next generation with God's wisdom and strength.

My friend Terry Bone addresses transitioning well with a heart of love for the church and its leaders and its mission. In this book, Terry takes his years of pastoral experience and combines them with his prophetic insight and teaching gift to provide an overview of how leaders must transition their roles and responsibilities well. This book will greatly benefit NEXT GEN and Older Gen leaders alike. I pray that you are challenged and affirmed by these words. I know that we need to get this right. This book will help.

May God help all of us as we find our part in the Race and run well!

MATT TAPLEY
Lead Pastor, Lakemount Worship Centre
October, 2017

PREFACE

This book is about making great transitions in life.

There is something called an *exchange zone* in track and field relay races. It's a well marked space on the track in which the baton must be passed from one runner to the next. In that zone, a lot has to happen in a short period of time. This seemed to me like the perfect metaphor for transitions. *We all pass through 'exchange zones' in life.* These are meant to be a place where desires are fulfilled and destinies are transferred. Time spent in exchange zones is brief compared to the entire race. We ought to know what to do *before* we get there as there's rarely enough time to adequately absorb all we need to know *once* we get there. As the saying goes, 'we must take advantage of the opportunity of a lifetime during the lifetime of the opportunity'.

As a Life Coach and Leadership Consultant, I often walk with people through some of the most important transitions of their lives. Typically these are talented young leaders in the ministry or business world who are looking for both a plan and a person to walk with them while entering the next phase of their life calling. My wife, Melissa, and I have also written and spoken extensively on the topic of 'family blessing', the practice of giving Spiritual blessings to the ones we love most.

At some point I realized that a common challenge was present in every situation. Parents who desire to pass on Spiritual blessings to future generations, leaders of a ministry or business who want to set up the next leader for success, and aspiring leaders waiting for their turn to shine, all need to master the art of transition. This involves more than just different people 'taking turns' doing the same thing. A successful transition includes a baton transfer. In real life, the baton represents the transfer of knowledge, wisdom, authority and even Spiritual gifts between current leaders and those who are called to be next in line.

So I created a couple of messages on how to 'pass the baton' between two generations of leaders. Everywhere I shared these messages, people kept asking for the notes. It was time to start the process of writing a book. I spent a couple more years making additional notes and collecting quotes. I sought the perspective of some outstanding young leaders within my community in order to broaden my perspective. I also served as an Interim Pastor for several churches in the midst of leadership transitions.

After all this, I hired a writing coach who helped me to distill a thousand pages of loosely connected notes into a more concise and compelling format. I trust that the result is an easy to read book that addresses important questions on this important topic.

If you find yourself currently in an exchange zone, may you receive practical guidance as you read the pages that follow. If not, then now is the right time to bank this knowledge for a future date. Either way, I pray the Holy Spirit will illuminate the truths you need to ensure that you make a great transition when the time is right.

ACKNOWLEDGMENTS

I want to thank four persons who have significantly impacted the formation of this book.

In order of ascending influence they are:

John Snelgrove who introduced me to Paul Scanlon's book <u>The Battle for the Loins</u>. Revelatory concepts from that book were foundational for parts of this book.

Anne Ames, my Writing Coach, who walked me through the long process of turning a thousand pages of disconnected notes into a concise readable format and went above and beyond the call of duty at times.

Melissa, my wife, who is the best text editor I have ever met. She is also a master at combining sweet encouragement with a kick in the pants when such action is truly beneficial.

Holy Spirit, my counselor. His voice, His persistence and His amazing ability to illuminate an idea have convinced me that He is a genius.

CONTENTS

PART ONE
Discovery

———

In this opening section, we will discover how life becomes an 'Amazing *Relay* Race' when differing generations meet in life's *exchange* zone. We will also discover how profoundly generational thinking will impact your important life decisions.

Chapter 1 introduces the 'Relay Race' theme and its three associated 'life-shaping truths':

1. Your personal destiny is a team event.
2. The baton pass defines the outcome of the entire race.
3. There is a way to create generational permanence in what you are called to do.

Chapter 2 identifies and celebrates the EMERGING GENERATION. This generation is producing a great number of potential World Shapers, whom we define as *persons who will noticeably influence and impact the sphere in which they live.*

Chapter 3 goes beneath the surface of success to discover the timeless truth of the idea of COVENANT. It examines how the 'thousand generation' promise God made long ago *is still relevant and powerful* for every follower of Jesus today.

Chapter 4 is a modern day account of restoring lost destiny. Using a lighthearted manner, Terry tells a story of how the amazing grace of God overcame generations of unbelief and negative patterns, *when just one generation* chose to turn back to God's ways.

CHAPTER 1

Your Amazing Race

Definition of a Relay race:

A track-and-field sport consisting of a set number of stages (legs), usually four, each leg run by a different member of a team...The runner finishing one leg is usually required to pass on a baton to the next runner while both are running in a marked exchange zone.[1]

Everyone loves a good race. As a young adult in the 1980s, I was in awe of the 'Golden Milers', an elite group of athletes who constantly set new world records for running the mile. But my favorite was the 26 mile marathon. It seemed so *extreme*.

Not so any longer. Since the 'X Games'[2] debuted in 1995, racing events have been getting longer, wilder and more dangerous. Pounding the pavement for 3 hours? Barely worth being called a marathon anymore. Now we have *week-long* mountain Death Races and Peruvian Jungle runs where broken limbs are optional but not unexpected. And how about the 'Yukon Arctic Ultra Marathon', a 300 mile winter endurance footrace in which you pull your own supply sled? In 2018, twenty-one people began the race in temperatures below -40C/F. Eleven days later, exactly one person crossed the finish line. The rest dropped out, losing not only the race, but also toes, fingers and even whole feet to frostbite![3] In spite of such stories, new extreme races are constantly appearing with no signs of abatement.

I would like to add one more to the list. I refer to it as The *Most* Amazing Race. Unlike the frantic competitions mentioned above, this unique race offers ample adventure without the broken bones or frostbite. And best of all,

---

1 retrieved May 2018 from https://www.britannica.com/sports/relay-race

2 The **X Games** is an annual extreme sports event hosted, produced, and broadcast by ESPN

3 reported in many news articles such as www.cbc.ca/news/canada/north/yukon-arctic-ultra-changes-1.4677313

you don't have to be an adrenaline junkie or extreme athlete to win! Many people with ordinary abilities have entered with low expectations only to experience the joy of standing upon the medal podium when it's over.

So what is this race? And why is it the most amazing one?

It is the Great Relay Race of Faith and Destiny. The Christian faith is often described as a 'walk' with God. That it is. However, when it comes to fulfilling your destiny, that special purpose for which you have been placed upon this planet, the New Testament seems to prefer the metaphor of running rather than walking. Followers of Jesus are called to emulate great heroes of the faith by *running the race* that is set before them.[4] The Apostle Paul also talked about *running his race* of faith.[5] Today's preachers use this metaphor to encourage perseverance using catch-phrases such as, '*Life is not a sprint, it is a marathon*' and, '*Keep your eyes on the prize, stay focused on Jesus!*'

> A relay race is the only
> event where you don't
> have to cross the finish line
> to win a medal.

But those messages miss one vital element. This Great Race of Faith and Destiny is not meant to be a series of solo runs where everyone gives it their best shot. It is actually a *relay* race. That one word makes a fundamental difference. A relay race is the only event where you don't have to cross the finish line to win a medal. Wrapped inside that pithy statement are some profound insights that have shaped my personal values and defined my destiny. I refer to them as life-shaping truths. Here are the top three:

Life-Shaping Truth #1
Your personal destiny is not a call to individual greatness - it is a team event.

Your life is not a solo run. Who you are today, what you will accomplish tomorrow and who you will eventually become, are all connected to others

---

4   Hebrews 12:1-2

5   2 Timothy 4:7

in the same race. This includes not only those you are currently running alongside, but *also those who came before you and those who will come after you*. Therefore every destiny is actually a shared destiny, passed from generation to generation. Understanding how this works requires a shift to what we call 'generational thinking'.

God always thinks and acts generationally. It is rooted in the way He views time.

Let's talk about that for a moment. Think of your life as a parade containing all the events you will experience within your lifespan. Because you have a ground level view, you are limited to experiencing the sight and sound of each event sequentially as it marches by. We call this 'time'. God, on the other hand, has the 'Goodyear Blimp' view of your parade.[6] From that vantage point, God can effortlessly view and access any portion of your parade at any time. Every action God takes in the current moment takes into consideration the entire parade. It is all NOW to Him. Not only that but He knows how each of the many parades connects to the next.

When we experience that same aerial view that God has, even for a few brief moments, we instantly realize that life's greatest prize is far larger than we can see from ground level. Every personal victory has generational impact somewhere down the timeline of history. Here's a stunning example: *Every time you lead one person to faith in Jesus Christ you may have changed the history of an entire family line.* You may have impacted thousands of lives! That thought dramatically increases the stakes when considering how and when to share your faith. The same dynamic is in play in the events preceding your life. You and I are benefitting from the faithfulness of those who went before us in ways we cannot comprehend this side of heaven.

Every life is limited by time and talent. Generational thinking frees your destiny from these limitations. Think of it this way: who has a better chance of winning a relay race, an *exceptionally talented* athlete who runs the entire four laps on her own, or four *fairly talented* runners running one lap each?

---

6   I was going to call it the 'God-year' Blimp but that pun is too terrible to even mention in print.

(I hope the answer is obvious.[7]) When your life is lived with the expectation of inter-generational success, that's when the possibilities become limitless.

Generational thinking doesn't come naturally when our days are constantly being chopped up into tweet-length conversations and endless Instagram posts. Today's tech-driven, hyperactive culture constantly spews forth information that may fascinate for the moment but serves no purpose in our lives next week. Even when not staring at a pixelated screen, our energy is often consumed by attempts to 'keep our boat afloat' in the midst of urgent family needs, work commitments or health issues. Making time to pause and reflect on the long term picture can feel like trying to stop that boat while shooting the rapids. Nevertheless it's worth the effort. Discovering how your personal destiny is connected to those who came before you and those who will come after you will give shape to your prayer life, your business life and your most important relationships.

Life-Shaping Truth #2
The Race is won or lost in the baton pass.

To understand the importance of the baton pass, let's contrast the relay race with other team sports competitions. In high school I ran as part of the cross-country team. Each school was permitted to have as many runners as they wished. However, only the top four finishers on each team count. The rest are ignored when tallying the total team score. So although it is technically a team event, it's really just a bunch of individual runners doing their best. As long as you have four good runners, it doesn't matter how bad the rest of your team performs (which is precisely why I 'qualified' for my school's team). Even a swimming relay requires only that the next swimmer wait until the previous one touches the wall. There is no physical connection between team members. They merely take turns trying to do their best.

---

7   just in case the answer is not obvious, it may help the reader to know that most Olympic relay teams complete four laps quicker than the individual world-record holder for the same distance.

Whoever currently holds
the baton also holds
the aspirations of the
entire team.

But the track and field relay has one unique element that must be completely mastered by everyone before anyone can feel the weight of gold around their neck: *the baton pass*. While brief in timing and simple in concept, the baton pass is challenging to execute. The transfer between runners takes place within a marked 'exchange zone'. The members of a track and field relay team have only one goal: *move the baton to the finish line*. It literally determines the outcome of the race. Therefore whoever currently holds the baton also holds the aspirations of the entire team. One Olympic sprinter describes it this way:

> *"In the individual event it's all about you and how you're feeling and how fast you can go. In the relay…you have the momentum from the other runners to help you. It no longer becomes about how fast you run but how fast you get the (baton) around (the track)."*[8]

When the baton pass is successful, every team member has the chance to share a spot on the winner's podium. When the baton falls to the ground, winning is impossible, regardless of how well any individual performs.

So, with respect to your own amazing race, *what is the baton*? It's not a shiny piece of hollow aluminum. Your baton is the *Spiritual authority* that you carry as a follower of Jesus Christ. It is a good kind of authority. It comes from heaven and exists for the purpose of serving others, never for manipulation or control. Day by day it can be observed in the amount of healthy influence you have in other people's lives. It's light to the touch, but weighty in power. In your hands, it has the ability to bestow not only God's presence, but also the accumulated wisdom and knowledge that the next runner in your race needs to succeed.

---

8   Anchor leg runner Bolade Ajomale as quoted in the article 'Life in the Fast Lanes' by Kerry Gillespie, Toronto Star Sports, August 11, 2017

How this actually works will become crystal clear throughout the pages of this book. We will continue to circle around this theme, showing how it applies to your faith, your family and your life calling, whether you are a CEO or the boss of nobody in particular.

I am astounded at how many leaders I have spoken to have put little or no thought into how their role will be transferred to the next generation. We have often treated the sacred batons of faith and leadership like a set of car keys left on the counter with a note for the next one who happens along.

Fortunately every generation includes a few leaders who think generationally and prioritize the baton pass. Here's one example from the life of Apostle Paul, the first-century pioneer missionary. Paul's desire was to preach the Gospel of Jesus Christ throughout the entire known world. Through his outstanding efforts, this Good News story had already taken root for the first time in many new lands. While en route to the ends of the earth, he was sent to prison where he would eventually die. From his 'death row' cell, Paul wrote a letter to his spiritual son, Timothy, announcing "I have fought the good fight, I have finished the race..."[9]

How could Paul assert that his race was finished when his major life goal was not yet fulfilled? Because his 'finish line' was not defined by task or location but by relationship. Paul had been intentionally preparing his protégé for such a time as this.[10] Paul knew that Timothy was ready and waiting in the 'exchange zone' with an open hand. As long as Timothy took the baton from Paul's outstretched arm, Paul's leg of the race was finished even though many more generations of runners would follow.

Life-Shaping Truth #3
Three in a row creates the opportunity for permanence.

When three generations *in a row* successfully pass along what they carry to the next generation, the momentum becomes *unstoppable* for generations to come. In the Bible, the number three is often associated with

---

9   2 Timothy 4:7

10   both through mentoring and the impartation of Spiritual gifts e.g. 2 Timothy 1:6

completion or fulfilment. This concept has an observable quality in life and in scripture.[11] Some sociologists have recognized that family traits or habits become ensconced around the third generation.[12] And in Major League sports, when a team wins a championship twice in a row it's called a 'repeat' but *three* times in a row is a *'three-peat'*. At that point you will hear them referred to as a dynasty. Three-in-a-row creates a momentum that draws even more top talent toward that team.

A *spiritual* three-peat can also represent the tipping point from individual destiny into a corporate dynasty. There is a famous three-peat family team in the Bible whose intergenerational story graphically illustrates our point. The backstory is that God had made a powerful 'family blessing' covenant with Abraham in which He promised to oversee the spiritual and physical welfare of every descendant of Abraham.[13] When God recruited Moses to deliver the enslaved nation of Israel, He began by revealing a new name for Himself:

> God also said to Moses, "Say to the Israelites, 'The Lord, the God of your fathers—the God of **Abraham**, the God of **Isaac** and the God of **Jacob**—has sent me to you.' "This is my name forever, the name you shall call me from generation to generation." Exodus 3:15

In contrast to some of the more formal names of God revealed in the Old Testament, *"I am the God of Abraham, Isaac and Jacob"* sounds more like a nickname between friends. Why would He insist on this new name? The purpose was to remind Moses that the 'family blessing' passed between these three generations was the fountainhead for God's faithfulness to all the generations that would follow. Forty years later, Moses reminded the

---

11   I am not a numerology guy but it is self-evident that the number three is significant in scripture. For example, the nature of God is completed by three distinct personalities: Father, Son and Holy Spirit. And the redemption story is completed in three parts; life, death and resurrection.

12   for a great example, try Googling 'Shirtsleeves to Shirtsleeves in three generations'

13   for a more in-depth look at the nature of the 'family blessing' promised to Abraham and accessible to everyone who believes, see The Family Blessing Guidebook, which Melissa, my wife, and I wrote together.

upcoming generation of this truth when he told them, "*It is not because of your own righteousness that you are going in to take possession of the land... the Lord your God will drive them out before you to accomplish what He swore to your fathers, Abraham, Isaac and Jacob*".[14]

Abraham, Isaac, Jacob and their wives faced unique battles and sometimes went 'off track'. The mistakes they made are shamelessly recorded in the Biblical narrative.[15] However, *each one was faithful to pass along the family blessing.* In every generation the blessing not only continued but increased. The fourth generation produced Joseph - someone who truly changed the world in which he lived. He carried such unstoppable favor that a murder plot, false accusations and jail time couldn't keep him down. Joseph's wisdom and favor shaped the destiny of a nation.

At that point in time, the blessing resting upon the extended family clan become a permanent fixture. The centuries long trials in Egypt didn't change God's intention or weaken His resolve. Today, over three thousand years later, no amount of rebellion from within, or persecution from without, has been able to destroy the nation of Israel.

Full credit for this goes to the faithfulness of God to His own spoken Word. But His promise also needed to be ratified by three successive generations of obedience. It was set in stone by the family 'three-peat' of Abraham, Isaac and Jacob. Their victory in the battle for permanence is still evident in the land of Israel today.

What does this look like today?

Turning now to a more recent example, I want to share with you the story of a man whose small victory in an obscure mountain village helped changed the course of Christianity in many nations. Between the two World Wars of the twentieth century, a simple carpenter in Romania prayed constantly for the Lord to allow him to lead at least one Jewish person to faith in Christ.

---

14   Deuteronomy 9:5

15   If you are not yet familiar with these three champions of the faith, perhaps you want to take time to read their four generation family story in Genesis chapters 12 through 50.

The problem was there were no Jews living in his village. One day a wealthy young Jewish atheist came to the village to recuperate from an illness in the fresh mountain air. The carpenter opened up his house as a convalescent home for this stranger and led the Jewish atheist to faith in Christ. The carpenter died a few years later, oblivious to the rest of the story.

The name of the Jewish man was Richard Wurmbrand. Over the course of the next three decades, Wurmbrand led thousands of people to Christ. After boldly confronting the atheistic Communist government in his own country, Wurmbrand became the first Christian to be thrown into prison for his faith by that new government. After fourteen tortuous years, Richard was ransomed by Christians from the West. In short order, he and his wife Sabina began a world-wide movement called 'Voice of the Martyrs' which as I write is helping Christians who suffer for their faith in dozens of countries around the world. *One rural villager in Romania ran his race and passed the baton of faith to one man.* Three generations later, the impact is still being felt around the world.

Closer to Home

My own childhood was devoid of the concepts we have been talking about. My parents never heard of terms such as 'family blessing' or 'Spiritual authority'. In our home the word 'blessed' was used as a substitute swear word, while the phrase 'kingdom come' was a slang phrase used as a warning that I would soon be punished (don't ask, it's complicated). Thankfully, my Heavenly Father assigned angels to watch over me from the observation deck of His blimp. Consequently, I became a Christian at 15 years of age, a Holy Spirit intervention in the life of an aimless young man who was heading for trouble. The process included multiple attacks on my unbelief using strategically placed neighbours and a runaway teen aged girl. An African-American named Humphrey Duncanson from Long Island, New York was used to complete the intervention on a never-to-be forgotten Friday evening in Northern Ontario.[16]

---

16   Humphrey was the guest Bible Teacher at a Bible camp which I had attended, so I thought, merely to develop my relationship with one or more of the female participants. Humphrey led me to Jesus that week.

My Heavenly Father subsequently arranged for a select few runners to meet me in the exchange zone of life and ministry. The leader of my first youth group, Bart Wiles, was mid-thirties when I met him. He was the first to pour in some of the family blessings I had missed early in life. He rewrote the script of what I believed possible for a kid like me. His passion for soul-winning marked me for life. Bart had huge plans for our growing youth group but his life was suddenly cut short by cancer before his thirty-ninth birthday.

The following year I landed at a church where the Pastor was legendary for thinking 'outside the box' of his generation. Pastor George Tunks was a true pioneer in ministry, planting churches from scratch, attracting new people of all social strata and imparting spiritual gifts into the lives of average people. George was a fearless risk taker, willing to go where others wouldn't as long as he perceived it to be a win for the Kingdom of God. Having recognized a call to ministry upon my life before I did, Pastor Tunks was willing to mentor me and place me in his pulpit on occasion even before I had formal Bible training. I learned much from him in those early days. To my disappointment, those days came to an end when my wife and I purchased our first home and moved out of town. Soon we lost touch with Pastor Tunks. Twenty-five years later, circumstances brought him back into my life and the bond between us resumed. Now in his nineties, Pastor Tunks was eager to finish his race well. He met with me one day and announced that he was conferring upon me what he called the mantle of his ministry. He prayed that I would pick up where he left off in the ministry of spiritual gifts for which he was renowned. Not long afterward George Tunks was 'promoted to Glory'. His act of faith bestowed upon me something invisible yet very real. Since that time, I have been privileged to see God's presence and power released upon many lives in many countries.

> You have been given
> authority to receive and
> carry a baton in three
> areas of life: Your faith, your
> family and your life calling.

I thank God for a small number of men from the previous generation who saw me as God sees me *and were willing to trust me with what they carried spiritually*. Humphrey, Bart, George, and a couple of others are the precious few who showed me the race course, handed me a baton and cheered me on. They saved me from years of aimless running. It proved to be a Great Exchange!

What About Your Race?

Are you aware of the areas in which you carry the baton of Spiritual authority? Maybe you have been running for years and are tempted to set it down quietly on the grass beside the track. Or perhaps you are still looking and waiting for a baton to carry.

Whatever your place in the race, be assured that *you have been given authority to receive and carry a baton in three areas of life*: Your faith, your family and your life calling. With respect to your faith, the authority you carry is the baton of the Gospel. For parents, it's your ability to impart not only the Gospel, but also a 'family blessing' to your children and children's children.

In the life calling or leadership arena, it is about recognizing and releasing the next generation of leaders to grasp the authority handed to them and take it to entirely new places. *It's critical that we get this right.* Those holding the baton cannot afford to cling to their positions of influence as if the baton itself is the prize. The destinies of others must not be put on hold while you wring out every last drop of self-fulfilment from your position of authority and influence. The generation of leaders currently emerging have 'world shaper' written across their hearts. Those of us who have been running our race for decades need to meet these potential heroes in the Exchange Zone *now* in order to accomplish a successful transfer of authority, gifts and anointing. The emerging generation is primed and ready to take what we carry to a whole new level. It's time to release them to become an unstoppable force in the earth!

CHAPTER 2

World Shapers on the Way

———

You say you want a revolution
Well… you know
We all want to change the world…
From the song Revolution
by John Lennon & Paul McCartney

On March 24, 2018 a diminutive African American girl stood on a make-shift stage, her eyes scanning across a crowd estimated at a quarter of a million people. With the wireless microphone held close to her chin, she spoke with as much volume and authority as her nine-year-old voice could deliver.

> *"My grandfather had a dream that his four little children would not be judged by the color of their skin but by the content of their character,"* Yolanda Renee King, granddaughter of Martin Luther King Jr., continued, *"I have a dream that enough is enough."*

The throngs had gathered in Washington D.C. for the 'March for Our Lives' anti-gun violence rally in response to a string of school shootings earlier the same year (in the USA). This spirited nine-year-old was just one of many speakers that day, and *all of them were pre-teens or teenagers.* Yolanda King then led the crowd in this impassioned chant she had prepared as *an eight-year-old* for the anniversary of her grandfather's death:

> *"Spread the word! … Have you heard!*
> All across the nation!
> We … are going to be!
> A great generation!"

Yes they *are* going to be a great generation!

They are the first generation of 'digital natives', able to navigate the internet since they could hold a spoon.

They are calling out hypocrisy found in my generation.

They are questioning our methods and moving our boundaries.

They are assaulting the status quo and sweeping aside time-honored traditions with a shrug.

> This new generation is also
> hungry for illustrations of
> integrity in the lives of the
> older generation.

I believe that, as long as the Word of God is not dishonored, that is what they are supposed to be doing! The emerging generation won't take 'no!' for an answer. They are hungry for change and willing to make it happen with or without the blessing of those who went before them. If you are over forty years of age and feeling uncomfortable with this then I have a word for you. *Get over it.* Ready or not, what looks abnormal to the previous generation is about to become the new normal. A new generation of world shapers is well on their way.

Famous Baton Passes from the Past
This new generation is also hungry for illustrations of integrity in the lives of the older generation. They aren't unwilling to be led, but they are unwilling to trust a generation of leaders who have produced far too many moral failures. They also refuse to view previous accomplishments as their gold standard for success. (After all, isn't this the definition of a relay race? The next runner receives the baton from the previous runner, and runs with it into new territory.)

Looking again at some famous Bible duos, we see that Joshua was not at all bound by the limits surrounding the life of Moses. Moses had taken the Israelites *out of* Egypt and *through* the wilderness but was unable to get them *into* the promised land. Moses even argued with God about that, for he desperately desired to finish the race he had begun. However, the Jordan River would become an uncrossable boundary line. It would also become an exchange zone as *Moses' finish line became Joshua's starting line.* Once appointed, Joshua marched the children of Israel through that river to the other side without working up a sweat (or even getting wet). Immediately he began the conquest of the promised land. Unburdened by past failures and filled with fresh energy, Joshua also carried a new anointing upon his leadership. With Moses' mentoring and blessing, Joshua was 'ready to rumble' and fully equipped to lead the next generation into new territory.

Moving forward several generations in the Old Testament narrative, we read that the prophet Elijah performed more miracles than anyone had since the days of Moses. His victory over the false prophets on Mount Carmel had begun to turn the hearts of the people back to God, yet as his life came to an end, the nation was still in the grips of a corrupt queen and king. His protegé, Elisha, held his mentor in great esteem, yet something rose up within him that said, '*Elijah's anointing wasn't enough to complete the task - there must be more! And I am going to have it!*' On Elijah's last day on earth, Elisha looked him in the eye and requested a double portion of the miracle anointing Elijah had been carrying. Elijah replied "*You have asked a hard thing*".[17] This is likely the summary of a much longer conversation. I imagine the full text of Elijah's reply may have sounded more like this, "*You want double my anointing!? No one has ever equaled the signs and wonders shown by my hand. Also the more I prophesied and performed miracles, the more trouble I received. Maybe you should lower your expectations. You can always ask, but you have about as much a chance of receiving a double portion as seeing me go up to heaven live in chariots of fire...*". The chariots did come and Elisha was heartbroken to lose the most influential person in his life. Yet he immediately got to work and began to exercise his new level of authority. 'Where is the Lord God of Elijah?' he cried out as he struck Elijah's fallen cloak upon the water. Putting that into modern vernacular, Elisha was saying "*Ok, let's see this new authority in action!*"

Joshua and Elisha did greater exploits *than* their mentors, but they couldn't have done greater exploits *without* their mentors. Moses and Elijah willingly facilitated a transfer of Heavenly authority to the next generation.

---

17 2 Kings 2:10

Consequently, Elisha and Joshua didn't miss a beat. They took the baton from the previous runner and *instantly picked up the pace.*

These examples are exceptional. More often, the history books serve up stories of failed opportunities and poor transitions. Today we are also hard-pressed to find examples of great transitions between leaders. And we have not yet arrived at the place where transferring the faith between family generations is the norm. I still hear far too many stories of adult children who do not desire to walk in the 'faith of their fathers'.

Success requires trust at both ends of the baton.

So this begs the question, what can bring the generations together long enough to enable a successful baton pass? The answer to that question came one Sunday morning to me from an actual track coach who heard me teach on this topic during a church service. Gordon Roddy used to coach relay teams at a local high school. The baton analogy profoundly spoke to him in ways I hadn't yet fully considered. His description of a winning relay team painted a perfect picture of what needs to happen between today's generations. Here's Coach Roddy in his own words:

> *"I found that* <u>trust</u> *was a key component in relay building. Four strangers will never make a good relay team even if they are good runners. Developing strong relationships between the members of a relay team is crucial to success. Without positive interpersonal ties between its members, relay teams will disintegrate when things go wrong.*
>
> *As for the race itself, runners racing into the exchange zone had to trust the next runner to take off at the right point in order to reach their maximum speed while still being inside the zone, and to then accept the baton. The outgoing runner had to trust the incoming runner to catch him/her and to blindly extend the correct hand back to accept the baton. Teams that developed trust often went far. Those that did not were seldom successful."*

Trust is the foundation that undergirds it all. The exchange zones are often crowded and confusing, with multiple hand-offs occurring simultaneously. Each runner must know what to expect from the one holding the other end of the baton. If the incoming runner does the job, the outgoing runner will feel the baton firmly pressed into his or her hand before they exit the zone.

To succeed in that environment requires trust *at both ends of the baton*. At one end trust is expressed by a willingness to let go at the right time. At the other end, it is seen as a willingness to wait just long enough to take hold of that which is being offered. Moses and Joshua had it. Elisha and Elijah had it. King Saul *didn't* have it. And David, the one waiting on him, paid the price. Saul was the first king appointed over Israel and he started out well. But Saul faltered when the rightful heir to the throne began to make a name for himself. Bursting onto the scene as a giant-killer, David's well-earned reputation only grew from there. It soon became apparent that David would not only become king, but also that he would eclipse the accomplishments of his predecessor. Rather than seeing this as God's plan to bless the nation, Saul became jealous to the point of obsession. Years of conflict ensued with an inevitable result. David became king anyway and by the time he died, Saul's reputation and legacy were demolished.[18]

David practised extreme honor toward Saul as an outward sign of his inward trust in God. He understood that an early start would disqualify him, not from being a physical king, but from carrying *the full weight of Spiritual authority* available in that role. So David waited arduously in the exchange zone unwilling to begin his leadership laps until, at long last, the baton of kingly authority was handed to him by those who buried Saul.

A story like that is brimming with applications for leaders and for families today. But before we return to the 21st century, I want to share the story of one more famous Bible duo that profoundly illustrates how to bless and release the next generation with the full authority that God intends.

---

18   I just compressed 20 chapters of the Bible into a few sentences. It's a fascinating read found in the book of 1 Samuel chapters 8 through 31

The main characters are two pregnant women, one middle-aged and the other a teenager. You may have already read their story, but this time think of it as two generations conducting one of the world's all-time great baton passes.[19]

> Elizabeth's home became
> an exchange zone where
> Mary received exactly what
> she needed to begin her
> own amazing race.

Mary was engaged to a young man named Joseph when her life was interrupted by a high-ranking angel named Gabriel. The angel announced that the Holy Spirit would do the impossible by causing the young virgin to become pregnant with the Christ child, Jesus. Gabriel declared that Mary was highly favored in God's eyes, but in the eyes peering at her from doorways in her small village, Mary would likely be seen as an adulterer, eligible for severe punishment under the religious law. Was there no one able to perceive what God was doing? Mary's only action had been to embrace the great thing that God had revealed He wanted to do in her life. Who would believe her story and understand her situation? Who could bless what God was about to do? There was at least *one* person, Elizabeth, Mary's older relative. The same angel had visited her husband, Zechariah, six months previously to announce that Elizabeth would have an improbable birth in her postmenopausal years. The baby would grow up to become John the Baptist, the forerunner of Jesus. Mary hurried to Elizabeth's home in the hill country with anxious anticipation. "Maybe Aunt Lizzy will understand me!" she thought. Her highest hopes would soon be fulfilled.

Upon Mary's arrival, Elizabeth burst into a prophetically inspired blessing declaring that Mary was carrying the Messiah. Elizabeth considered the event a great honor saying "Why am I so favored, that the mother of my Lord should come to me?" She understood that what Mary was carrying went beyond anything Elizabeth would ever deliver to the world. Elizabeth knew by the Holy Spirit that her child would spend his life pointing to the

---

19   see Luke chapter 1 for the full account

ministry of Mary's Child. Elizabeth's spiritual perception was matched only by her selflessness. Elizabeth didn't use Mary's visit as an excuse to tell her own story or dish out advice. She didn't begin the visit by saying "*Well young lady, I also heard from the same angel, and I too am expecting. If I can do it at my age, you'll be just fine.*" Elizabeth was focused upon Mary. She was fine with the fact that Mary's pregnancy was the bigger story. Elizabeth had an *improbable* pregnancy but Mary had an *impossible* pregnancy. As a result, Elizabeth's home became an exchange zone where Mary received exactly what she needed to begin her own amazing race.

Thirty years later their children would share a similar moment. When speaking of Jesus, John the Baptist declared, "He must increase, but I must decrease".[20] At that time John was the most famous person in the nation. But he knew that *now* was time for the greater One to take center stage. And so at the height of his popularity, he willingly surrendered the attention and Spiritual authority he carried. He pointed at the One who would pick up the national revival where John left off, and turn it into a redemption story. (Perhaps John inherited that attitude from his mother.)

Now let's pull the lessons we learn from these stories into the 21st century. We have some 'Marys' among us right now. They may not stand out in a crowd, but what is happening on the inside is profound. Their faith levels go beyond the norm. They have had personal encounters with the Holy Spirit and heard God's voice in private. They have said 'yes' in their heart to challenges that the previous generation has written off as impossible. As a result, they carry within them a revelation of what God wants to do in the world around them. Who else can see what they see?

In some instances, close friends or family have rejected them for what they carry. Misunderstood and unblessed, they still nurture a hope that there is someone who is spiritually in tune and selfless enough to help them deliver to the world what they are carrying. When they come to my generation for counsel or advice, they don't want us to use the conversation as an opportunity to tell our own story. Their desire is not for a fifty or sixty-year-old cool companion who dresses and acts like them. They don't need a buddy, they need an 'Elizabeth'.

---

20   John 3:30

Someone who looks at them and recognizes them according to the Spirit.

Someone who prophesies about who they are in God's eyes.

Someone who calms their anxiety and affirms their future.

Someone who blesses them to go beyond the limits of the previous generation.

One Someone Can Be Enough

Here's a timely word regardless of which end of the baton you find yourself holding: *Just one 'someone' can counterbalance all the negative voices by speaking truth on God's behalf.* Elizabeth was that one someone for Mary, and her actions more than counterbalanced an entire village full of unbelieving friends and family.

In spite of showing great bravery in battle, future King David was dishonored by his brothers and overlooked by his father. Yet when the prophet Samuel recognized David according to the Spirit, a life-pattern of being neglected was overturned. *One anointed person* launched David onto the pathway from shepherd boy to great king.

Looking at it from the other end of life, it may only take one baton pass to enable you to turn apparent failure into a stunning success. Moses tried to take a whole generation into the promised land, but only two made it; Joshua and Caleb. Joshua led the entire next generation into the fulfilment of Moses' deepest desire.

Someone Please Stand in the Gap

When the Baby Boomers were young rebels, our parents coined the phrase 'Generation Gap' to refer to that empty void between the older and younger generations. We could not see eye to eye on many matters, both important and trivial. It felt as if neither side was willing to budge. We eyeballed each other and said 'come on over to my way of doing things'.

It's a place where destinies converge and dreams are fulfilled.

Today I see that gap becoming an overlap, one which contains a richly-textured Exchange Zone of ideas and shared goals. It's a place where destinies converge and dreams are fulfilled. We all need to intentionally spend time in that zone for the relay to succeed. It's time for some counter-cultural revolutionaries to rise up and do life together so that models of The Great Exchange become more commonplace. A few things will need to occur for this to happen. Here's a word for people at both ends of the baton.

A Word to My Generation

Wake up and smell the coffee! Don't accept false finish lines and wander off the track. Your race is not over at retirement. Don't allow your life to become a game of 'Trivial Pursuit'. Someone is waiting for you to hand them the baton. For those of you who never left the track, don't treat that baton like it's the prize. Don't forfeit an enduring reward in order to eke out a few more years of status and entitlement. Your greatest accomplishment in life will occur when you, like Moses, give some of your authority and hard earned wisdom to the next generation.

A Word to Potential World Shapers

You're already awake and smelling the artisanal organic fair trade coffee. You care about the earth in ways we should have long ago. You are passionate about social justice issues. You are wary of our identity politics. And you have a deep desire for authenticity in relationships. I do offer this warning though: cafe conversations will never change the world. Your insightful opinions are meant to be the starting line not the end game. You will never fulfill your destiny if you limit your circle of touch to your own kind. We can help you fulfill your destiny, but only if you'll come and meet us with open hands in the Exchange Zone.

I See a New Day

I am hoping that by the time many of you read these words that they will sound obvious. I see some tangible signs of a new day rising. I see successful baton passes happening more often between family members and leaders of all kinds in recent days. I believe that a *new normal* characterized by blessing and honor is already taking shape, where the emerging generations naturally lean towards the wisdom of the previous generation; one where the incoming runners recognize and call forth the greatness of the outgoing runners.

The great intergenerational relay of faith, of family and of life calling is becoming the Most Amazing Race. Ever.

CHAPTER 3

A Thousand Generations

─────

You can count how many seeds there are in an apple, but only
God can count how many apples there are in a seed
Robert H. Schuller[21]

God always thinks generationally.

He keeps track of time by counting *generations*, not by counting *years*. The Old Testament narrative recorded the history of Israel, not as a list of dates and events, but rather as a repeating cycle of generations linked together by God's faithfulness. Looking forward from Old Testament times, the Psalm writers say:

> "*Your years go on through all generations*" Psalm 102:24

> "*The plans of the Lord stand firm forever, the purposes of his heart through all generations!*" Psalm 33:11

Looking backward from New Testament times, the Apostle Paul said that the mystery of the Gospel was hidden by God, not for centuries, but '*for ages and generations*'.[22] God always acts with future generations in mind. When we do the same, the potential impact of one life becomes limitless.

Consider the astounding six-generation legacy of Jonathan Edwards, the famed 18th century preacher. During his lifetime, Edwards became a master theologian and gave leadership to the initial stages of a nationwide spiritual awakening[23]. He and his wife Sarah had 11 children and apparently taught

─────

21   adapted from BrainyQuote.com. Xplore Inc, 2018. 5 April 2018. https://www.brainyquote.com/quotes/robert_h_schuller_121372

22   Ephesians 3:4-5 and 8-9

23   The following appears in Wikipedia under Jonathan Edwards: "Edwards is widely regarded as one of America's most important and original philosophical theologians...Edwards played a critical role in shaping the First Great Awakening, and oversaw

them well. Around 1900, a Pastor named A.E. Winship traced their lineage and discovered among their 1400 descendants, the following could be found: [24]

- more than 100 lawyers, 30 judges

- 13 college presidents, and 100 more professors

- 62 physicians

- 100 clergymen, missionaries, and theological professors

- 80 elected to public office, including 3 mayors, 3 governors, several members of congress, 3 senators, and 1 vice president

- 60 who had attained prominence in authorship or editorial life, with 135 books of merit

- 75 army or navy officers

- A Comptroller of the U.S. Treasury.

- "practically no lawbreakers"

The above list reveals that the lifetime accomplishments of one young couple named John and Sarah was *multiplied many times over* in the generations that followed.[25] Even so, the list above cannot begin to measure the full impact of the family blessing that began with their obedience. Today it is rare for families to have 11 children like the Edwards did. The main takeaway

---

some of the first revivals in 1733–35 at his church in Northampton, Massachusetts." (accessed March 2018)

24   There are many exaggerated versions of this list out there, and most include a contrast with a man named Max Jukes. I had to turn to a secular source to acquire a version unembellished by preachers who are overly-eager to make a point. Psychologist Robert Frick has done an excellent job of parsing fact from fiction. I have used information from his research with permission. See http://rfrick.info/jukes.htm

25   It ought to be noted that according to Winship, "Much of the capacity and talent, intensity and character of the more than 1,400 descendants of the Edwards family is due to Mrs. Edwards."

here is not the number of successful people per se, but rather the *number of generations* that kept producing successful people. The fact that this family blessing juggernaut was still on a roll after six generations is what makes this story so remarkable.

> World-shaping dreams
> are usually the result of a
> shared passion that propels
> a single pursuit across
> several lifespans.

Who can Change the World?

World shapers are rarely made in one generation. There are exceptions, but most often, the kind of people who bring actual change to the culture in which they live (and not just talk or tweet about it) are the product of multiple generations of successful baton passes. That's because world-shaping dreams are rarely possible to achieve within a single lifetime. They are usually the result of a shared passion that propels a single pursuit across several lifespans. Martin Luther King Jr.'s famous 'I have a Dream' speech was the product of two generations of sacrificial civil rights activism. His father and mother, Martin Luther King *SR.* and wife, were both descendants of slaves and sharecroppers. MLK Sr. faced vicious opposition and paid an enormous price to pioneer a civil rights movement. He was willing to be a lone voice in a vortex of racism in the hostile south. Both father and son looked forward to a future day when their people would not be judged by the 'color of their skin but by the content of their character'[26]. Neither completed the task. When MLK Jr.'s nine-year-old granddaughter Yolanda quoted those very words at the March for Our Lives rally two generations later, they carried the weight of *four* generations of people who paid the price and passed the baton. As I listened and watched Yolanda speak, the power on those words made her sound like a pint-sized world shaper. Oh how we need Yolanda's generation to pick up the baton and go beyond the reach of her forefathers!

---

26   I assume the reader is acquainted with the 'I have a Dream' speech delivered by Martin Luther King Jr. from the steps of the Lincoln Memorial in Washington D.C. on August 28, 1963

Private sacrifices of one generation bring public blessing to the next generation.

World-shaping churches are usually the product of multiple generations of leadership as well. The sound that has emanated from Bethel Church in Redding, California has already impacted the lives of thousands of leaders around the world, including several members of my family. The personal times of ministry I received there have been pivotal for my missions ministry and personal prayer life. It comes as no surprise to me that the Lead Pastor of that church is a *fifth* generation Pastor on his father's side and *fourth* generation on his mother's side. As I crossed the lobby of Bethel one day, I noticed a sign placed in honor of the Lead Pastor's father that read '*his personal victory has become our corporate inheritance*'. Those words landed on my soul like a truth bomb! The private sacrifices of one generation bring public blessing to the next generation. No wonder there is such a powerfully abiding presence of the Holy Spirit upon that house of worship.

Now, if you and I were discussing this in person, I would expect to hear you ask, "*Why is it so uncommon for us to see examples of multi-generation success today?*" I think the answer is found primarily in our unrealistic expectations. Unrealistically *high* expectations, or unrealistically *low* expectations. Let me explain.

Today's emerging generation is being fed a constant diet of hyper-positivity which claims 'you can change the world!' The truth is, even billionaire humanitarian superstars like Bill and Melinda Gates have had a tough time trying to change the world within their limited lifespan.[27]

Yet many young leaders are living in a constant state of hyper-expectation. They are constantly amped up and expecting a world-shaking breakthrough at any moment. Too often they are merely being set up for deep discouragement

---

27   I once was seated beside one of the Gates foundation's employees on an overseas flight who shared with me the immense ongoing challenges associated with their goal of eradicating malaria from the planet.

later in life. What's missing is the understanding that *their destiny dreams will span several generations.* Just like the first-century disciples, their vision is sound but their timing is off. Peter, Paul and friends believed that they were preparing the whole world for the sudden return of Jesus Christ. Well, actually, they were. It's just taken a few more generations than they imagined.

Meanwhile, the middle-aged generation typically suffers from unrealistically *low* expectation levels. Ongoing struggles in their work and family lives can dramatically lower their energy levels. Decades of disappointments may appear to mock the great promises found in Scripture. Sadly, too many moral failures by public leaders have also deflated the expectations of many. Consequently, we view families such as Jonathan and Sarah Edwards' and churches like Bethel as shining exceptions that go far beyond what is *reasonable to expect* for the rest of us.

Covenant Contains the Cure

The power contained in the agreement called 'covenant' contains the cure for what ails our soul. It contains the ability to both calm the anxious heart which is trying too hard and also to heal the heart poisoned by cynicism. The word covenant is a legal term meaning inviolable agreement, *a promise that cannot be broken.* We have two main covenants in the Bible. The *New* Covenant is the promise of eternal life through the sacrificial death of Jesus. That's the only covenant you need to know about in order to live forever. You don't need to follow all those strange rules from the *Old* Covenant. But, don't throw out the baby with the bath water. The rules are set aside, but not the promises! The Old Covenant has not been *abolished*, it has been *fulfilled.*[28] The difference between these two words matters. All the rules and regulations associated with the Old Covenant have been fulfilled by the blood sacrifice of Jesus. Meanwhile, there are promises from that period which are still relevant and beneficial to your life. There is one particularly powerful promise to which I want to draw your attention.

The World's First Summit Meeting

That promise was made in the first 'summit' meeting between God and humanity. I am referring to the conversation between God and Moses near the summit of Mount Sinai. The people of Israel had recently experienced

---

28   Matthew 5:17

a miraculous escape from Egypt but had little understanding about this God who had delivered them. They knew about His 'deeds' but Moses was about to learn His 'ways'.[29] These ways included rules written in stone that we call the Ten Commandments. Also written in stone (in the subtext of the second commandment), was a promise to bestow unending favor that would overcome any sinful inheritance within families. Sinful family patterns were said to affect three or four generations. In contrast, God revealed Himself as one *showing love to a thousand generations*. (Exodus 20:6 and 34:6-7) In other words, God's love was not only powerful enough to forgive an individual's sins, *but also to clean up the mess sin makes and leaves for the lives of those who follow later.* When left unchecked, our sinful habits have a way of repeating themselves in the lives of our children, grandchildren and sometimes even great-grandchildren. The Thousand Generation covenant cancels that effect as soon as one generation turns back to the Lord. This covenant reveals the heart of an all-loving, awesomely patient Heavenly Father. It became a recurring theme of the Psalmists, especially King David as he composed worship songs for the Tabernacle:

> "*He remembers his covenant forever, the promise he made, for a thousand generations.*" [30]

The children of Israel understood this covenant. They constantly drew upon the record of God's past faithfulness in order to inform their future expectation. Through Jesus Christ, God the Father has made the same unending commitment to you and to me.

Discovering Faithfulness

Some people, like me, came to faith in Christ without any sense of spiritual heritage. As a young Christian my family and I were at odds. They didn't trust my new faith. I felt like I had been voted off the island and was set adrift to find my own way. I became used to 'toughing it out' on my own.

After marrying Melissa, my life was connected to a living example of the kind of spiritual momentum generated by multiple generations. It was strangely

---

29   Psalm 103:7 says 'He made known his ways to Moses, his deeds to the people of Israel.'

30   Psalm 105:8 (NIV)

wonderful to see how her five siblings and their children gravitated towards serving God regardless of the circumstances that surrounded them. When she inherited her mother Sylvia's Bible, Melissa discovered just how strong this current was running through her family. As well worn and loved as an old shoe, Sylvia's Bible had hundreds of notes written in the margins. Melissa was reading Psalm 78:3-7 from it one day which says:

> *"...things we have heard and known, things our ancestors*
> *have told us.*
> *We will not hide them from their descendants;*
> *We will tell the next generation the praiseworthy deeds of*
> *the Lord, his power, and the wonders he has done.*
> *...he commanded our ancestors to teach their children,*
> *so the next generation would know them,*
> *even the children yet to be born,*
> *and they in turn would tell their children.*
> *Future generations will be told about the Lord.*
> *Then they would put their trust in God*
> *and would not forget his deeds but would keep his*
> *commands."*

Next to this Psalm, Sylvia had inserted a list with the names of *nine generations* of followers of Jesus from her family line beginning with her German ancestors. Here's that list:

- Johann Gerd *told* Gerd *who told*
- Johann Friedrich *who told*
- Gerhard Friedrich *who told*
- Herman Heinrich *who told*
- Theodore August Friedrich *who told*
- Sylvia Charlotte *who told*
- Rick, Becky, Peter, Matt, Melissa, Ellen *who told*
- 18 grandchildren *who told*
- ?

Beginning in the 1700's and finishing with her grandchildren born in the late 1900's, the baton pass of faith and family blessing had spanned two centuries, crossed an ocean, traveled through multiple countries, spoke several languages and survived *four* major wars. Reading those verses from Psalm 78 is inspiring. Seeing the names of our own family beside them takes it to the next level.

The '?' represented the great-grandchildren Sylvia was hoping to live long enough to meet. She treasured the thought of one day blessing one of her grandchildren's children, holding the young one in her arms. The closest Sylvia came to this was to bless her first pre-born great-grandchild Abby, while still in our daughter's womb, during a family Christmas gathering. Sylvia went to spend eternity with her Lord three weeks later.

We are now well into the tenth generation from Johann Gerd where the blessing on Melissa's family line is a prevailing force. It's been relayed through so many lives that the battle for permanence has long been won. Yes, each person must choose the faith for themselves and willingly surrender to God's call upon their life. The fact is that those who have neglected to do so are a small minority. I believe that's because the current of this generational blessing is so deep and wide that it's hard to stay out of the river.

Beyond Marriage and Family

Beyond the family arena, whatever great thing you are called to do, the same principle applies. Great solo efforts in business or ministry are not meant to be 'one and done'. In the right environment, the authority given to one leader can be passed on and becomes unstoppable.

> People who aren't parents
> are still in the mainstream
> flow of this covenant.

Even people who aren't parents are still in the mainstream flow of this covenant, with many opportunities to pass the baton. Jesus never married or had biological children while he walked the earth. We know that Jesus poured his life into twelve ordinary guys and they took it from there. That turned out pretty well, didn't it?

I also know another single man in his thirties who knew how to pass it on. My first youth leader, Bart Wiles, never married or had children of his own, yet he poured his heart and soul into the lives of many teens. Hundreds of people found faith in Christ through Bart even though his life was cut short through illness before his fortieth birthday. Thirty years later, six of us he had discipled gathered at a restaurant. All of us were serving the Lord, and pouring our lives into the next generation. Four of us were employed in full-time ministry. That's quite the legacy for a man who left us so soon!

Personalize the Promise

To acquire God's perspective, we need God's point of view - the aerial view. Every once in a while we need to take a short ride in that parade blimp hovering overhead. Reading Bible stories, biographies or perhaps our own journal can lift us up to where the air is clear and the view of God's unending covenant love is spectacular. The truth is that God's faithfulness to you and those you love will indeed last for a thousand generations. Dare to personalize this truth. Before you read further, think about the impact of *your* life three generations from now. What do you think will be said about you? What would *you like to be said about you* if you had a choice? Give yourself permission to DREAM BIG for sixty seconds…

What comes to mind? *That's* generational thinking.

Perhaps you want to make your own list to insert in the Bible pages beside Psalm 78:3-7. Your generational blessing list may be short or non-existent, but let me encourage you that some of the greatest family stories are written by God's grace intervening when an inherited blessing is nowhere to be seen. That would be my story, and it's coming up next.

CHAPTER 4

When God Closes the Gap

------

*The secret things belong to the Lord, but the things revealed
belong to us and our children forever'*
Deut. 29:29

I do not believe in the good old days. I am far more interested in what God is doing next. However, if the stories of what God has done in the past were not relevant to our lives today, then we could toss out most of the Bible. This chapter contains the *astounding story of revival* in our church, in our family and in our community. Like some well written mystery novel, three seemingly separate stories came together like three strands in the same cord. It was not fiction, rather it was the hand of God revealing hidden things and writing the story upon our hearts. I have included several conversations so that you can experience these events the way I did. We begin with the strangest day of my entire ministry life...

> It was not fiction, rather
> it was the hand of God
> revealing hidden things.

Buried Spiritual Treasure Uncovered
Hamilton, Ontario Feb 24, 1995

As the hotel elevator doors parted, an elderly man from the American midwest stepped out looking somewhat like Mr. Greenjeans from the old kids TV show *Captain Kangaroo*. Oh no, I thought to myself, this is the man who will be speaking at my meeting? Twenty-five years later, I can still see the suspenders that hitched his pants a little too high, the farm fresh plaid shirt, and the ample amount of grey hair and eyebrows, all of which needed a good combing. If his outfit could talk, it would have said, "Let's bale some hay!" He looked around to see who might be there to meet him. I turned away quickly pretending not to see him and did a lap around the lobby to buy time. To understand why I was nervous, let me give you the backstory.

A fellow Pastor had told me that this man was very prophetic, especially in what the Bible calls 'word of knowledge'. I was still undecided about the issue of modern day prophets, but I was intrigued by his reputation. However, this prophet rarely visited Canada, so I hesitantly accepted the opportunity to have him speak at our church.

My reputation as a Pastor was already taking some hits due to the unusual events unfolding at our church services. For seven months, the Holy Spirit had been radically impacting people with astounding results. The fruit was amazing - bodies healed, families restored, marriages revived and more - but sometimes it was *noisy* fruit. Let's just say it was quite demonstrative. Some people groaned in prayer, wept, laughed out loud or fell over. It was unlike anything I had ever seen. But these same people were worshiping and praying like never before and attendance and offerings were *way* up. What's not to like about that? Well, some people just couldn't get past the physical responses that didn't fit the traditional worship service grid. They were 'worried about us'. Ironically, no one seemed to be worried about us the previous year when we couldn't pay the bills or fill the pews even if everyone had stretched out horizontally!

Now it was a full house with non-stop Holy Spirit manifestations meeting after meeting after meeting. Our church was being transformed into a growing, vibrant Worship Centre attracting people from all over the region. (We had actually changed the name to Lakemount Worship Centre a month before this all began, which in hindsight was a prophetic act.) Nevertheless, we were being shunned by certain folk who thought that all this noisy stuff was 'in the flesh'. My response was "Hey it's the same 'flesh' that used to sit there silently staring at me - I would rather have that flesh doing whatever it can to worship God!"

OK, back to the hotel lobby. That day we were having multiple meetings, kicking it off with a gathering of regional leaders featuring this particular prophetic person. David Mainse, TV host of 100 Huntley Street[31], among other renowned persons, was supposed to be attending. Frankly, I was afraid

---

31   100 Huntley Street was by far the most watched Christian Talk Show in Canada for over thirty years and often enjoyed higher ratings than most secular TV Talk shows in Canada

of what they might think of me and our church. I took a deep breath and prayed a short silent prayer for everything to work out. I introduced myself, picked up the prophet's luggage and made small talk on our way to the car. As soon as we pulled away, this kind elderly man looked at me, broke into a fatherly smile and began to relay what the Holy Spirit had revealed to him. A lot was said during the twenty minute drive to our church. It was all important, but these are the words that will be forever etched into the retina of my soul:

Prophet: *'Son, God's been talking to me today about you and your church."*

Terry (inside voice) : Here comes the prophetic, I hope it's good!

'There were great Holy Spirit events that happened on your ground in the last century".

Not bad so far, could be encouraging.

"The secret to your ministry is from the late 1850's"

Oh no, from encouraging to weird in two sentences!

'The anointing doesn't evaporate, it hides under the rocks and the trees'

uhhhhhh… blank stare

'You don't follow me, do you, son?'

Of course not. What do you expect when you say weird things?

Me (out loud for the first time): *"No, I'm sorry I don't"*

Like Jesus unveiling the meaning of parable, the prophet began to speak plainly,

'What I am saying is that the prayers prayed and the promises made in a certain location don't just disappear after a while. They don't fade away or lose their power. They remain in the spiritual atmosphere, for generations if necessary, waiting for their fulfilment. Waiting for someone to pick them up.

'And son, I know there were promises made and prayers prayed over your land. I believe you have you the authority to pick up where others left off and walk in the fulfilment of those promises.'

Me (out loud): *"I will certainly look into that"*

Me (inside voice): 'Oh man, what is going to happen in the meeting today?!'

Prophecy, Pepsi and Toilet Paper

The Leaders' meeting that day was unusual both in the format and in the astounding accuracy of this man's 'word of knowledge.' It included an extended time in which people were called individually from the crowd to sit in a chair in front of the prophet, who then spoke what he felt the Holy Spirit was telling him for that person. I purposely did not introduce anyone we brought forward as a means of testing the accuracy of what he had to say. What transpired was remarkable. The prophet had a word for David Mainse that later proved highly accurate and helpful. (David reminded me of that word several times in subsequent years, describing it as an important milestone for him.)

The *real test* would come from my wife. Melissa can smell a phoney a mile away and she wanted to make absolutely sure that what we were receiving was genuinely from God. I was under strict orders that her identity be kept secret from our guest. When my wife sat in the chair, the prophet immediately blurted, *'Oh here is someone with the gift of helps! You're the one who makes sure there is enough toilet paper and the one who gets the man of God a Pepsi.'* Yes, for real. That was his 'word' for my wife! Well, wouldn't you know, just before she left our house for the meeting, Melissa had a random thought to check the supply closet to ensure there was enough toilet paper. Then en route she picked up a large Diet Pepsi to help me get through the long day of meetings. When our prophetic friend said those words, Melissa's eyes went wide. The prophet noticed this and said, *"Sorry dear, did I offend you? I was just making a little joke before I started to prophesy."* Yes, for real. He was speaking a word of knowledge even when he was just trying to make conversation. Evidently, his spiritual gift was in full gear that day!

After watching him in action for hours, I pondered everything in my heart. It was *real* but how could I be 100% positive that this gift came from the Spirit of God? My heart was settled after reading 1 John 4:1 which says, '*Beloved do not believe every spirit but test the spirits to see whether they are from God*'. The answer popped right off the page. We are told to test the *spirits* not test the *methods*. My comfort level with a man's methods cannot be the litmus test for authenticity. Rather it is to be determined by the spirit which motivates his work. Though he was eccentric, this prophet had focused on Jesus, displayed a father's compassion, included the message of the Cross and inspired us all to pray with greater faith. And … he never once mentioned money. When I brought up the subject, he didn't seem to care what he was paid. My mind was made up. This man was legit.

The Grimsby Campground

Now it was time to test the prophet's word about the spiritual history of our land. The first thing that came to mind were some stories of an old Methodist campground in our hometown. The dates were vague, but it seemed like a good starting point.

So off to the Grimsby Museum I went and by 'coincidence', I arrived during the week they happened to be featuring a scale model of the Grimsby Campground from the 1800s, replete with artifacts, pictures and original news articles. Directions to the site led me to a unique lakeside subdivision called Grimsby Beach. It was a mish-mash of by-law breaking hundred year old homes on tiny lots. The actual gathering spot for the camp meetings was at the corner of what is now called Temple Lane and Auditorium Circle. In the center of Auditorium Circle was a circular patch of grass about 100 feet in diameter where the tabernacle had stood for the campground meetings. A cairn of stones mortared together stood in the middle. I walked up to it and read the plaque:

The First Methodist
Camp Meeting
was held here
in 1859

The prophet was right on with the date!

I hurried back to the museum to find some more clues to the mystery of what could be still 'hiding under the rocks and the trees'. I read everything I could get my hands on over the next few weeks. Here's a bulleted list of significant facts I uncovered from museum documents:

- In the absence of churches, during the early 1800's, itinerant Methodist Preachers called 'Circuit riders' had ridden throughout our region (the Niagara Peninsula) traversing woods, rivers and bramble bushes to serve the spiritual needs of the saints and bring new believers into the fold. Today their circle route takes less than two hours by car. Back then, it took two *days* on a horse.

- In 1859 a generous man severed 18 acres of prime lakeside wooded land and gave it to the Methodists to establish a permanent meeting place.

- On the day the first tree was cut to clear the meeting space, all present bowed and dedicated the land to the work of God for evangelism and spiritual refreshing.

- The first series of meetings in August 1859 were preceded by much fasting and prayer.

- The first sermon preached was based on the scripture **1 Kings 18:41** 'I hear the sound of the abundance of rain'.

- Over the next decade, weeks of meetings were held each summer and a full blown spiritual revival took place in the region, with the campground serving as the epicenter.

- Grimsby's population was 1,200 at the time. Yet up to 4,000 people gathered at the campground during meetings. This was decades before the first automobile rolled into town. They came by horse, rail and boat.

- Eyewitness accounts spoke of meetings that were marked by hilarious laughter, singing in the Spirit and after-service prayer meetings lasting well into the night.

- The campground became a year-round affair with a strong emphasis on leading children into a place of personal faith in Christ.

- Many churches were planted in the region as a result of what happened in the meetings.

- Eventually, the spiritual fervor waned, and the land was sold and turned into an amusement park around 1901.

- Around the time the camp was being sold, more than one person felt the Holy Spirit was saying that the land would once again be used for the Kingdom of God, *only next time it would be permanent.*

Now I understood that our town had previously been the center of a true spiritual awakening. People from that period of time prophesied that it would one day resume. Four generations later, our church, located two kilometers from the edge of the campground, had begun to experience a similar outpouring of God's Holy Spirit.

More pieces of the puzzle would soon appear, without any prompting. A couple of weeks later, I was in another town sitting in a crowded church service when the visiting speaker stopped, pointed at me and declared, "*Son, your scripture is 1 Kings 18:41.*"

That was the same scripture used in the inaugural sermon at the campground. It refers to Elijah's words when his prayer to end the drought was answered. It is often used as a metaphor for spiritual outpouring, i.e. we can pray and receive God's refreshing when all around us seems spiritually dry. To top it off, after hearing me share some of these insights, a member of our deacon board, Len Houser, said to me, '*Check this out, I am actually a direct descendant of the brother of one of the Grimsby Campground's board members*'. Indeed he was. Fourth generation down the line.

Spiritual Heritage Revealed
Hamilton, June 1995.

The Campground story would prove to be just one of the strands in a three-fold cord. The second was about to be revealed. Around the same time as the

Campground story was unfolding, I was sharing with someone that I was a 'first generation' Christian and as such did not have a spiritual heritage. All at once, a very clear thought came into my mind, the kind I have learned to recognize as the Holy Spirit. Loud and clear I heard:

"STOP that, You are dishonoring Me!"

I realized that the Lord was actually rebuking me for speaking an untruth. So then I prayed, "I'm sorry for that Lord, but what *is* my spiritual heritage? I don't see it."

Days later I was on a long bicycle ride through Hamilton and decided to stop in at the only living relative of my paternal grandfather. Uncle Gord was the youngest of seven siblings and the only one to make a home on our side of Lake Ontario. Everyone else in the Bone clan lived in the Greater Toronto area. We were chatting on the porch, when out of the blue his wife asked, "*Would you like to look at the family tree?*" Our family *never* talked about this kind of stuff. My grandfather, when asked, would only say of the past, "*We were horse thieves*" (and for many years I believed him). Now I was staring at a handwritten sheet of paper that listed the ancestors on my father's side for five generations. I discovered that my great-grandfather was actually named *John Wesley* Bone. Now that was interesting! The original John Wesley was the 18th century founder of the Methodist movement. Not only was he a great teacher, but during his preaching, many people had powerful personal encounters with the Holy Spirit. By the 1800s his movement was the dominant Protestant expression in England and among immigrants in Canada. *The inescapable conclusion was that three generations ago my family were Methodists who knew the Lord!*[32]

Cycling home, I felt a strong impression that the Lord was bringing the Campground story and my family story together. A little more sleuthing revealed that John Wesley Bone had been a faithful worker in the Methodist Church where he lived, and near the end of his life moved not too far from the original site of the campground. That seemed like a strange coincidence.

---

32   As this book was being written, we discovered the location of the unmarked grave of my great-great-great grandfather, Thomas Bone, north of Toronto, and the associated information confirmed that my family were indeed English Methodists.

I prayed, "Lord what are you saying to me?" The answer and the manner it came to me are entirely subjective. However, looking back I am still certain that I was hearing correctly. I felt a strong impression that the Holy Spirit was saying "*Terry, your family served the Lord until John Wesley Bone's generation. Prayers were prayed that have remained unfulfilled due to the wandering of three generations including you and your siblings. My will is to restore the call upon your family. It's yours to pick back up if you want it.*"

> There was a baton hiding under the rocks and the trees which my Heavenly Father had brought into plain sight.

This represented a major revision of my sense of identity. No wonder I was dishonoring the Lord by (ignorantly) proclaiming that I had no spiritual heritage! I wasn't merely a kid from a dysfunctional family who found the Lord. I was the inheritor of generations of promises and prayers sowed into my life by faithful ancestral family members. The ground I was standing upon contained an unclaimed spiritual heritage from my Methodist family *and* from the Methodist revivals. There was a baton hiding under the rocks and the trees which my Heavenly Father had brought into plain sight. It was waiting for me to pick up and run the next lap in the unstoppable, intergenerational plan of God.

When God Closes the Gap

For the first time, I understood that my family story and the phenomenal events at our church were somehow interconnected. Sure, we were experiencing what many would call 'revival with signs following'. We were praying, praising and meeting with great fervor and frequency. But this sudden unveiling of the intergenerational purposes of God led me to believe that there was something more we could do that would prevent us from becoming one more example in the long list of short-lived revivals. How we could we turn our Holy Spirit *visitation* into a *habitation*? How could we ensure that the Thousand Generation promise would not only revisit us after four generations, but remain permanently upon our lives and land?

Once again I stumbled over the answer. This time it was revealed through a brief prayer I received at a conference around the same time. A word of knowledge spoken by a trusted traveling minister was the key. He prayed "*Lord I believe that you are giving Terry's church gifts of repentance*". That statement, combined with recent study I had done on the Biblical account of the prayer of Daniel, became another 'Aha!' moment for me. Daniel was a faithful leader who had not personally engaged in any of the rebellious behavior common to his people. *Yet he confessed the sins of his people using the pronoun 'we'* in order to remove God's judgement against the entire nation (i.e. their captivity).[33] Daniel's prayers were important and effective, opening the door for God to return the people of Israel to the Promised Land. We call this 'identificational repentance'. Now I understood that one important step in the process of creating a permanent dwelling place for the Holy Spirit would be to pray like Daniel prayed.

It wasn't hard to identify some sinful patterns of my own family line. I named them in a very simple prayer of confession. Then I asked the Holy Spirit to separate me in every way from any mental or spiritual influence that might be lingering in my life from those ungodly patterns. I asked that the Holy Spirit would reveal any other relevant items, and He did.

Now, what about the campground? *What had permitted the Holy Spirit's fire to be extinguished?* I researched the history of the Campground's later years to find the answers. I discovered that the second generation of leaders had become embarrassed at the unrefined and boisterous nature of the revival. They wanted to make it neat and tidy. One eyewitness looking back twenty-five years later said, '*We're too sophisticated for that old-time religion today'*. That was said in 1900![34] When I shared these insights with the Lakemount leadership team, they were determined to never become *that*

---

33   See Daniel chapter 9. The underlying principle is that individual sins must be acknowledged by the individual sinner, but corporate disobedience can be confessed by anyone connected to the corporate group. Until this confession is made, the devil has a 'right' to prevent the corporate group from experiencing the full blessing of God. Once the sin is acknowledged, God's blessings can be freely bestowed upon that group.

34   My main source for quotes like these about the Grimsby Campground come from a book written by Harriet Phelps Younan, the niece of the Campground's spiritual leader, Noah Phelps. There is one extant copy in the Grimsby Museum. I was not permitted to remove it so I dictated parts of it and wrote them out later in longhand.

sophisticated. We confessed the sins of the previous generations of leaders who had permitted pride to cause them embarrassment over the work of the Holy Spirit. We sealed our confession with a prayer march from the center of the Campground worship site to our church, finishing with Daniel-style prayers of repentance on behalf of those who had led the Campground away from its original intent and ardor. We declared that we would never again permit the wells of the Holy Spirit to be blocked or dry up on 'our land'.

A quarter of a century later, it is my joy to still attend this church, no longer as the Pastor but as a member. It's a thriving regional hub of worship, prayer and spiritual activity, where the Word of God is believed and preached. The wells are wide open and full of Living Water. Ministries that were birthed here in the 1990s are still impacting the world today. Several newer ministries also have national and international influence and more world shapers are on the rise. Hopefully we're good to go for another 900 generations, or until the Lord returns.

More than She Asked or Imagined

There is one remaining strand to weave into this threefold cord of church, family and community. At that time, God was also about to 'close the gap' in the community, especially at the local High School, by taking unanswered prayers from the past and bringing them to rest upon our generation of young people. To understand how extraordinary it was that my own family members would play a role in this story, let me give you a thumbnail sketch of my family's spiritual dynamics. My four grandparents had well over twenty siblings in total and most lived in the Toronto area. They were a party-hearty and secretly dysfunctional lot that all got along surprisingly well. (Perhaps it was because alcohol consumption was the preferred method for putting the 'fun' in dysfunctional.) Just two or three were regular churchgoers and *only one* understood what it meant to be 'born again' to a new life in Jesus. That one was my grandmother's twin sister, who always referred to herself as 'Your Dear, Dear Auntie Marj'. She laughed often and possessed the quickest wit of the bunch. My conversations with her usually included stuff like this:

'*Hey Auntie Marj how old are you...for real?*'

"*Can't tell you kid, but I have one foot in the grave and the other on a banana peel.*"

Underneath the humor there was pain. Auntie Marj and her husband Art's only child, a son named Robert (Bob), was reluctant to serve the Lord as a teenager. As I said, we all lived in Toronto, but Auntie Marj and Uncle Art had moved *way out of the city* to a town on the south side of the lake called Grimsby. Their home was a few steps away from the Public High School where Bob attended. Auntie Marj, encouraged by her Baptist prayer group, prayed constantly for her unbelieving son and his companions as she looked out at the school from her window.

Unfortunately, Bob died in a car crash at 20 years old. The lack of knowing whether or not Bob had made peace with God worried Auntie Marj for as long as she lived. Her sense of anguish over this matter were her last words to me. As Melissa and I stood beside her deathbed, my dear, dear Auntie Marj passed from this life to the next life holding my hand. In her other hand was list of questions about her unanswered prayers. At that moment we had no idea that one of the answers would be played out in the context of our own life and ministry.

Twenty years after Auntie Marj went to be with Jesus, Melissa and I were called to pastor Lakemount Worship Centre in that same town of Grimsby. We looked at every house available for sale in town and the only one that gave us peace as we prayed about it happened to be located forty yards from Grimsby Secondary School (GSS), the same school attended by Auntie Marj's son, Bob.

Fast forward another seven years. Our children were now attending GSS. Lakemount Worship Centre was still experiencing the phenomenal fruit of the Holy Spirit outpouring. One of our daughter's unchurched school friends came to a Sunday service and gave his life to the Lord. Talk started getting around in the school about it. A couple more friends checked out our services. We sent people to the school grounds before dawn to pray and read declarations of faith. I recall that these declarations included: "*There will be true Spiritual revival with fruit that remains!*". In September, all Heaven broke loose. For a period of seven glorious weeks there were new GSS students arriving at our church each Sunday. Soon they filled the front two pews - yes, the *front*. We had unsaved, nearly saved and newly saved teens dancing in the aisles every week. Our people loved it, even the seniors. Our backyard pool became a favorite hangout for these new churchgoing teens. Granted, some of them just came along for the ride, but for several, the experience was authentic and the fruit has remained: one is serving as a Pastor today. I later discovered that during these weeks, other churches in the area also experienced an influx of GSS students. It's impossible to quantify the entire spiritual impact of those days, but even what we saw at the time was profound.

I am sure that many other people have prayed for the students of GSS over the years. I am also convinced that the God Who Closes the Gap had stored up Auntie Marj's prayers and *three generations later* released them with more powerful effect than our dear, dear Auntie had ever imagined. Marjorie nourished a hope until the day she died that her years of prayers would lead her own son to follow the Lord. But God had a much bigger plan in mind all along. My children are the fourth generation from Marj and her sister Dorothy (my maternal grandmother). The God who keeps His covenant of love for a thousand generations was preparing to avenge the works of the enemy by doing abundantly more than anything Marj had ever asked or imagined in her tear-filled prayer times.

Like a dam that bursts after the water has been held back too long, the answers to long forgotten prayers not only revived the fourth generation of one family line, but directly impacted a couple of dozen more family lines. Who can tell how many will be impacted in the generations that are yet to come?

Think about it one more time with me. We're talking about...

A Thousand Generation Promise that makes every failure become temporary and redeemable.

A Father who records and responds to *every* prayer that's prayed in faith, even when the answer is delayed for three or four generations.

A Redeemer who can reshape any short-term loss into long-term victory.

Our God is able to restart any race after the baton has been dropped, even after a delay so long the tall grass hides it from view.

He provides Amazing Grace for an Amazing Race.

PART TWO
From Destiny to Dynasty

———

Part Two is devoted to understanding the unique set of challenges faced by each of three generations on the road to creating permanence. Each leg of a relay race has unique elements depending upon the shape of the track where the baton is being passed. Likewise, each generation of believers will face unique challenges in their faith relay.

These principles apply not only to faith but also any form of leadership.

Chapter FIVE provides an overview of predictable battles the three generations will face on the pathway to permanence.

Chapters SIX through EIGHT deal with the individual challenges of each generation.

The First, or *Pioneer* Generation, fights the *Battle for Dominion*, the right to rule.

A pioneer is called to establish something new by leaving the comfort of familiar culture.

The Second, or *Bridge*, Generation fights the *Battle of the Bridge*,

A second generation person is called to connect the founders with the future. They take the newly established culture passed to them and link it to the generation that follows them.

The Third, or *Occupier*, Generation fights the *Battle for Permanence*.

A third generation leader or believer is called to capture the available momentum from the previous generations and turn it into an unstoppable force for the generations that follow.

In <u>Appendix A</u> you will find a point-form summary of how the three generations compare and contrast with each other.

CHAPTER 5

Know Your Battle

———

It's not enough to do your best,
you must know what to do and then do your best.
Ed Goodman

Whoever coined the phrase 'What you don't know can't hurt you' was wrong. Maybe even *dead* wrong. Just ask the skydiver who forgot to attach his parachute. Ignorance is not bliss, for it begets a confidence that lacks knowledge and can be downright dangerous. The truth is, what you don't know or can't see is often what *can hurt you the most*. I'm sure Edward J. Smith would back me up on that. He was Captain of the ocean liner *Titanic*.

In warfare, setting an ambush is an effective tactic which can give a smaller or weaker force the upper hand. However, *knowing* that an ambush is coming means it's no longer an ambush. Remove the element of surprise and you remove the enemy's advantage. As the cartoon action hero 'G.I. Joe' used to say, *"Knowing is half the battle!"*

Every race includes a battle of some kind. It is no coincidence that the word most often used for "race" in the New Testament original Greek language is *agona*. It can be translated as "fight" or "battle" as well as "race", depending upon the context[35]. Paul deliberately uses *both* meanings when addressing his son in the faith, Timothy, from his prison cell:

"I have fought the good fight (agona), I have finished the race (agona) …" [36]

You can't have a race without a battle. The crucial question is '*what battle will I face next?*' You cannot prepare for a battle you do not expect.

---

35   The Greek word agona appears at least eight times in the New Testament and can be translated as 'struggle' or 'race'. On five occasions scholars have discerned to translate agona as race. Four of those reference the life of Paul or those he discipled.

36   2 Timothy 4:7

> ## Remove the element of surprise and you remove the enemy's advantage.

Same Race, Different Battle

Each new generation of leaders face new challenges not encountered by the previous generation, even if they are leading the same endeavor. Let's go back to our track and field relay for a quick illustration. A relay race is *not* four repetitions of the same thing. Sports reporter Kerrie Gillespie describes it like this:

> "To succeed in the 4x100-metre relay takes a lot more than just four fast runners on the track. It takes runners with *a specific skill set for each leg of the relay* and, despite the event's name, each leg can range from as short as 80 metres to as long as 120 metres. It takes teamwork and precise timing to get the baton around the track …"[37]

Gillespie goes on to say how the first leg requires someone who can explode from the starting blocks, the second leg requires speed endurance and the third leg is best run by a curve specialist. The fourth, or anchor leg, is often reserved for the fastest runner. A wise relay coach knows what to expect at each bend in the track in order to maximize performance and ensure successful baton exchanges. The gold medal is reserved for the team that anticipates the next challenge and executes well.

The Apostle Paul appears to have anticipated the shifting battlefront for the next generation of leaders to follow him. The Second Letter to Timothy is the final letter we have from Paul and it is written from prison. Much of the letter focuses upon preparing Timothy to continue what Paul had started. As a pioneer missionary, Paul had faced much opposition. The list of troubles included flogging, beatings, stoning, shipwrecks, thievery, hunger, cold,

---

37   From the article <u>In the chaos of the 4x100 relays even the best can be beaten by the baton</u> by Kerrie Gillespie Toronto Star sports section on-line archives at www.thestar.com August 11, 2017

sleeplessness, false accusations, prison and more[38]. Knowing that Timothy was soon to assume some of his leadership duties, Paul was not interested in rehearsing his own previous battles. Instead he chose to discuss the *future battles* that he was sure Timothy would face. Paul predicted that "the time will come when men will not put up with sound doctrine...they will gather around them a great number of teachers to say what their itching ears want to hear".[39] He knew that new challenges from within the church would soon arise. With prophetic insight, Paul helped set up Timothy for success by giving him an early warning of what was waiting around the next bend in the race. *That's my idea of a Great Exchange*!

As I look around today, I see the odd example of this combination of self-lessness and foresight which produces generation-spanning success. Yet it is the *exception* rather than the rule.

Take my family for example. You may recall in this book's fourth chapter that there was a time when my ancestors knew God and served him. What they didn't seem to know was how to pass it on to the next generation. My great-great-grandfather George Wesley Bone named his son *John Wesley* after the famed 18th century evangelist and founder of the Methodist Church.

John Wesley Bone was a Lay Leader in His Church.

James Wesley Bone, his son, considered himself to be a Christian because he was baptized as a Protestant, and was faithful to the Orange Lodge.[40]

Robert Wesley Bone, his son, considered himself to be a Christian because he occasionally attended church and put money in the offering plate.

Bruce Wesley Bone, Robert's oldest son, considered himself to be a Christian because he wasn't Jewish.

---

38   2 Corinthians 11:23-28

39   2 Timothy 4:3

40   The Orange Lodge was an anti-Catholic Protestant Organization popular in the early twentieth Century

Terry Robert Bone, (that would be me) considered himself to be a non-Christian, and attempted to author his own religion (which had only one follower) until he became born again.

My family was pretty good at passing down the name of a religious hero, but not at passing along the faith he represented.[41] What were families like mine missing that allowed the faith of our fathers to melt away into oblivion? Simply put, we weren't aware that we were actually in a spiritual battle for the eternal destinies of our family. And when the signs of battle appeared, we tried to minimize them or wish them away.

My family's experience was by no means unique. The signs of cultural change were completely misread by the parents of my generation (the so-called Baby Boomers). As a result they were utterly unprepared for the seismic shift in culture that occurred in the 1960's. Rather than provide guidance for us, for the most part our parents became entrenched in their old ways. Like a crack in the ground that suddenly opens up during an earthquake, an unexpectedly large 'generation gap' appeared. Few saw it coming and it was generally mishandled by those on both sides.

Three Generations, Three Battles

Now we have come to the crux of the matter. For any important endeavor to become 'unstoppable', it must overcome unique challenges in three successive generations. I want to reiterate that this truth applies in different arenas of life. For example, an old adage in the business world – "*shirtsleeves to shirtsleeves in three generations*" – describes the propensity of family-owned enterprises to fail by the time the founder's grandchildren have taken charge. The data support the saying. According to the Harvard Business Review, a mere 10% of family-owned businesses remain active for the third generation to lead.[42] A successful businessman friend of mine says that in his industry there is a saying about family wealth that goes like this: "The first generation *makes it*, the second generation *enjoys it*, and the third generation *squanders it*".

---

41   Ironically I am the only male in five generations to NOT be named Wesley, yet I became the first to discover who Wesley was and what he believed.

42   from an online article at <u>hbr.org</u> Jan-Feb issue 2012, by George Stalk Jr. and Henry Foley entitled 'Avoid the Traps That Can Destroy Family Businesses'.

Exceptions to this rule occur only when those in leadership have learned to adapt to a changing environment.

> For any important endeavor
> to become 'unstoppable',
> it must overcome unique
> challenges in three
> successive generations.

Henry Ford's new motor car company was hugely profitable by the second year of operation. Forty years later, as the leadership was assumed by his grandson, Henry Ford II, the company was almost bankrupt. The challenges faced by grandfather Henry as he cobbled together his first quadricycle[43] in a Detroit coal shed were different than those that presented themselves to grandson Henry. It was time to adjust to the new reality. So new products were developed, new innovations made and the company got back to its winning ways. Perhaps you have heard that Ford still manufacturers vehicles today? Many other automakers don't. Evidence of their existence is found only in history books and scrap yards.

Let's go back now and have another look at God's 'three-peat' championship team of Abraham, Isaac and Jacob. They all passed along the same promised blessing, yet they each faced unique challenges based upon their position in the race.[44] God gave Abraham the promise of a huge family blessing. The trouble was, Abraham and Sarah, his wife, were childless. Nevertheless, the call to create family was upon them and a price needed to be paid to turn that dream into a reality. The long and winding paths of each of the four generations is the main subject of Genesis chapters twelve through fifty.

---

43   The name of the first automobile prototypes.

44   What I share in this chapter has it origins for me in Paul Scanlon's book *The Battle for the Loins*. Paul clearly lays out the premise that the first, second and third generations of faith each have unique battles - the first is the battle for the 'loins', i.e. influence over successive generations, the second is the battle of the bridge and the third the battle for permanence. Thanks Pastor Paul!

Enfolded into the story are nuggets of truth that illustrate the divergent battles faced by each generation. Here is the movie trailer version:

> Abraham was a pioneer in faith. The Bible calls him *'the father of all who believe'*.[45] He and Sarah had to leave their country, extended families and old culture to establish a new monotheistic faith in an entirely new setting. All they had to go on was a 'word from God', an unseen promise.
>
> Their son Isaac had a different challenge. He was called to *stay* in the land of his family, not leave it! He had to apply the call and vision of his father to a more stationary lifestyle and prepare the ground for future generations. He experienced supernatural assistance and provision for that task.
>
> The next in line was Jacob, who almost blew the whole plan up in everyone's face by trying to steal a blessing that was going to come to him anyway. Jacob was an exceptionally talented and shrewd businessman. His first challenge was to embrace his blessed inheritance of identity and destiny[46]. Jacob's second battlefront was for purity. His own deception was the root of the family discord. For a period of time, Jacob was a man on the run, avoiding his brother's death threat. He spent the next twenty years or so learning how to do it *God's way* rather than relying upon his own wits.
>
> It all came together in the fourth generation. Although the enemy tried to take out the entire family - one son - *Joseph*, became a national leader and saved the rest of the family from famine and certain death.

Whew… that was 38 chapters packed into a few paragraphs. Did you digest it all?

---

45   Romans 4:11

46   revealed to Jacob in a dream at Bethel where he saw the ladder extending to heaven. See Genesis 28:10-15

No worries if you didn't. The next three chapters in this book will make it clear. Each chapter outlines the unique challenges of a specific generation to make a successful baton pass. Just knowing these will help you 'fight the good fight' and run your race to win. It will also help you to assist others to fight *their* good fight and run their race well.

CHAPTER 6

The Pioneer Generation

Dreams are free. Goals have a cost.
Usain Bolt[47]

Definition of a Pioneer: A person who is among those who first enter or settle a region, thus opening it for occupation and development by others.[48]

If you are too young to have parents who grew up during the Great Depression (1930's) or the 'war years' that followed (1940's), then consider yourself blessed. Oh my, the stories my siblings and I endured at the kitchen table are legendary! Like the one about my mother's father who, unable to afford a car, resorted to crawling to work uphill on his hands and knees during an icy winter's day. As far as we could tell, these stories existed solely for the purpose of making us feel guilty for not having to suffer. Most of the stories began with the ominous phrase '*When I was your age…*'. We children noticed that, over time, the legends kept growing: "*You want a ride to school!? When I was your age, I had to walk ten miles to school in cardboard shoes and it was uphill both ways!*". A friend of mine's parent told him, "*Yes son, we had 'running' water, if we were willing to run a mile to the creek to get it.*"

Pioneers Leave the Old to Establish the New

At the source of every exaggerated tale is a true story. And the truth is that earlier generations did have it tougher than us, especially those who were actual pioneer homesteaders. When I sit in the plush seats in my home church on a Sunday, sipping on a latte before the worship service begins, *I must never forget the price that my spiritual forefathers paid* to bring the Gospel to the nascent nation of Canada. For those who left their homes, and their land to establish a new way of life in a new land, the price paid was extreme. Those who first come to mind are the Methodist Circuit Riders who brought

---

47   At the time of writing, sprinter Usain Bolt was still the world record holder for 100 metres and three time Olympic Gold medal winner at that distance.

48   From Dictionary.com accessed June, 2018

the first real wave of the Gospel to Upper Canada[49] on horseback. These men and their wives left the relative comfort of their homes in established cities and trekked through wilderness in order to establish a base of faith in a new land. The following is excerpted from my wife Melissa's research paper on this topic:

> "At that time (late 1700's), Upper Canada was a vast wilderness... 'Travelling on horseback, in all kinds of weather, over the length and breadth of the immense circuits... they were men of heroic type.. Wilderness roads, of dubious merit at their best, became miry nightmares after rainstorms and throughout the spring. Horses, buggies and sometimes preachers were swallowed up by 'oceans of mud'."[50]

Some even faced persecution for preaching the Gospel:

> "The first recorded Methodist preacher in Niagara was a Major George Neal, a native of Ireland and a member of the British Army. He formed the first class meeting of worshippers in Niagara Falls in 1788. "As Methodism was seen as a dissenting movement from the established Church of England, Major Neal was threatened with deportation by his commanding officer if he did not desist...he continued to preach but was sometimes pelted with stones until the blood flowed down his face"."[51]

Countless missionaries have faced similar challenges. Famous names come to mind like William Carey and Hudson Taylor who left their families and their homeland with the call to disciple a far-off nation. Just getting there

---

49   Before the current provincial boundaries were established, the area now known as Southern Ontario was called Upper Canada, as it was upstream along the St. Lawrence River. Quebec, situated further downstream was referred to as Lower Canada.

50   Melissa Bone - from her research paper on the Methodist Circuit Riders of the Niagara Peninsula with quotes from *The Garden of American Methodism*, author William H. Williams

51   Melissa Bone - ibid

took months. Thousands more lived, suffered and died to create a beachhead for the Gospel in unreached territory. They remain nameless and faceless to us but are well known in Heaven.

Pioneers Live by the Sound not the Sight

The runners of the first leg of a relay race have no visual clues to guide their start. They train themselves to respond instantly to the *sound* of the starter's pistol. Likewise, spiritual pioneers have little to rely on as they begin their journey other than the sound of God's voice to their soul. There's no manual or YouTube 'How To' video to assist them. They must become experts at *living by faith, not by sight*.[52] Abraham is our consummate example. To fulfill the call of God upon his life, he was instructed to leave his country, his culture and his cousins without knowing where he would be putting down new roots. He had rejected the 'polytheistic' (many gods) belief system of his culture to embrace one Almighty God who then told him, *"Leave your country, your people, and your father's household, and go to the land I will show you."*[53] When he and his entourage arrived in the new land they established a new way of life, including a whole new way of worship. Living in a promised land without a promised child, Abraham and Sarah waited for decades for the visible evidence of what they had been told.[54]

> Pioneers must become
> experts at living by faith,
> not by sight.

The original Methodists who made the arduous wilderness trek to Upper Canada from New York and Pennsylvania had also heard that inner voice telling them to head for a northern wilderness. Obedience to that word required great physical sacrifice since there were no real roads to get there.

Our church, Lakemount Worship Centre, was begun by a man named Alf Cowell, a true spiritual pioneer who heard God's voice to start a 'Spirit-filled

---

52   Paul's words from 2 Corinthians 5:7 'for we live by faith not by sight'

53   Genesis 12:1

54   For example Genesis 12:1, 13:14, 15:1,4, 17:9,15 Chapters 18 and 22 record whole conversations between God and Abraham.

work' in the growing town of Grimsby. He would often drive through the town with tears streaming down his face under the effects of a 'burden for souls'.[55] In 1965 Alf stepped out and with the assistance of his nephew John Dalgleish (and wife Marg), started meeting in a local elementary school. Neither were professional pastors. John was a police officer and in those early days Alf took no salary for his efforts. Three generations later, what Alf Cowell and John Dalgleish saw in the invisible realm is very visible and dictating the traffic patterns on the Grimsby North Service Road every Sunday.[56]

Pioneers Build New Altars

When pioneers establish new places of worship they must prioritize the altar over the tent. Let me explain. The altar represents spiritual worship and the disciplines that go along with it. The tent represents all the material possessions associated with a home and family. When Abraham reached the promised land, the first thing he did was to set his new priorities in order.

> "He *pitched* his tent...and there he *built* an altar to the Lord
> and called on the name of the Lord" "(Genesis 12:8)

Note the wording - Abraham '*pitched*' a tent but he '*built*' an altar. Which sounds like more work? Setting up a prefab tent of animal skins and wooden poles or lugging large stones a long way to one spot and lifting them up on top of each other? Right. The altar. A tent is designed to be flexible, movable and replaceable. An altar is strong and stationary. It may even outlive the one who built it. Thus we have a picture of Abraham's priorities. *The tent would follow the altar all through his life.* Not the other way around. We see the contrast between Abraham and his nephew Lot:

> '*Lot lived among the cities of the plain and pitched his tents
> near Sodom*'(Gen. 13:12).

> 'Abraham moved his tents and went to live near the great trees
> of Mamre...*where he built an altar to the Lord*' (Gen. 13:18).

---

55   As told to me by Alf's nephew John Dalgleish.

56   At the time of writing, Lakemount is a thriving large church with three generations of the John Dalgleish family attending Lakemount, including 92 yr old John himself.

Lot pitched a tent near a great stone city which offered a higher standard of living. In contrast, *Abraham's life revolved around a standard of worship, not a standard of living*. Abraham would become very wealthy but continue to live as a semi-nomad, frequently moving his tent to the location where he was called to build an altar. Stones were reserved for building altars, not houses.

Abraham's battle was for the 'right to rule'. Rule what? He would never sit in regal authority over the physical land. However, Abraham did win the right to rule over *the spiritual atmosphere* that would hover over both the land and his descendants. We know this because in Genesis 18:18, the Lord says that Abraham was chosen to "*direct his children and household after him to keep the way of the Lord.*" The word translated '*after*' means '*coming later in time*', i.e. his descendants.

> ## The right to rule begins by giving up your rights.

How did he win this right? Abraham gave up the most fertile land to his self-centered nephew Lot. Abraham selflessly walked away. Ironically, by giving up the chance to personally profit from the land, he won the right for his descendants to possess it all! Later on, he also gave up the right to keep his promised son given to him by God. Abraham understood that the right to rule begins by giving up *your* rights.

Like all pioneers, Abraham could see what was not yet visible. He built an altar to rule a nation. His personal obedience became his family's corporate inheritance, establishing a covenant for a thousand generations. The following generations would not have to repeat the battles that Abraham fought. They would have a new set of challenges to face.

Pioneers Create Critical Momentum

The initial runners in a relay have to create their *own momentum* from a standing start. Pioneers in any endeavor face the same challenge. For example, the founder of a new company may have nothing more to build her business upon except some start-up capital and the power of an idea. The momentum for all forward movement must be generated from within.

Many famous historical figures could be used to illustrate this point both in the business world and in the world of faith. However, I thought it would be more helpful to the average person to share my own story as an ordinary 'first generation' follower of Jesus.

When I became a Christian, I was bucking an entrenched family system. As the first one in my direct family line to serve the Lord in several generations, I was effectively walking the path of a pioneer. I needed to separate myself from the habit patterns of my family. My parents wanted me to abandon this new weird lifestyle for a more balanced life, which roughly translated meant 'why don't you party on the weekends?'[57] I had no strategic plan in those early days. The voice of the Lord to my soul was my guide. I was willing to pay a high price to escape my old ways and embrace a new way of living. And I desperately desired to be free from the sense of unworthiness I carried with me at all times. Success came by trading some of the normal pursuits of young people my age for what I will call extreme discipleship. I recall going on prayer walks for many hours at a time and memorizing whole chapters of the Bible (especially Romans 8). Four or five days a week were filled with Bible studies, prayer meetings and door-to-door evangelism.

A second generation believer would not have needed such an intense schedule, but it's what I required to escape the gravitational pull of my family system as well as my own bad habits. Although I didn't see it at the time, I was developing a lifestyle where the tent would always follow the altar, not the other way around. At that time, I knew that I was winning the battle for my own soul. What I didn't realize until many years later, was that *I was also winning the battle for the right to rule over the spiritual inheritance of my family line.*

A few years later, I married an eighth generation Christian. That also helped me establish a new family system! Melissa and I have always given priority to the 'altar' over the 'tent'. We have pitched our tent where God has called us to serve. We have not suffered for this. We are blessed in both our ministry and our home life. Our children are having to fight their own battles, as their leg of the race is different than ours. However, we're certain that the blessing

---

57   I am pleased to say that all family opposition to my faith has long since dissolved.

being sent down the family line through our children and grandchildren will continue for countless generations.

CHAPTER 7

The Bridge Generation

I want to be the bridge to the next generation.
Michael Jordan

In a 4x100 relay race, the second runner is the first one in the race to both receive and give away the baton. The second leg serves as a 'bridge' between the first leg, which is a straightforward sprint, and the third leg which is run mostly on curves. The same principle applies to our great relay race of life. Whether it has to do with sharing your faith or building a business, the second generation represents a vital link between its founding and its future.

Bridge Under Attack

In wartime, bridges are of utmost importance. 'Blow the bridge' and an entire operation grinds to a halt. 'Secure the bridge' and the whole operation moves forward. In the winter of 1945, the massed armies of the Allied Forces were advancing across Europe to reclaim land taken by the Nazi Army. Soldiers retreating across the Rhine River had blown up every bridge, effectively stopping the Allied forces dead in their tracks. However, early one foggy March morning, a lone scout aircraft spotted the Ludendorff bridge[58] still intact! Immediately the Allied Commanders rushed resources to that location. Engineers hurried onto the bridge and disarmed explosive devices moments before they were to be detonated. Both ends of the bridge were secured. Over the next ten days, the bridge became a special target of the enemy and finally collapsed from constant shelling. However, *by that time, enough personnel and equipment had made it across the river that a permanent stronghold was established* on the other side. Victory was now assured.

This wartime story provides a great metaphor for life. All the self-sacrifice and hard-fought victories of a pioneering generation can end up as mere stories on the bookshelf if the second generation does not secure a bridge to

---

58   The Ludendorff bridge crossed the Rhine River at Remagen, Germany. Today there is a small museum at the former footings which honors both sides who fought there and celebrates peace.

the future. When a new-found faith is beginning to transform a family or a new marketplace ministry is making inroads into the community, the enemy of our souls can still halt all future progress if he can somehow take out the bridge. Therefore it's of no surprise when a second generation believer or leader encounters great difficulties. *They are considered to be special targets by the enemy of our souls.*

Abraham was a sojourner, but Isaac was a settler.

A Salute to the Second Generation

Sandwiched between two exciting life stories of his pioneer father Abraham and his son Jacob, the account of Isaac's exploits in Genesis seems rather short and uneventful.[59] You could be forgiven for thinking his contribution is the least significant in the intergenerational family blessing. That would be a great mistake. Isaac's life served as a vital link between the former days and future ways of his family line. The new family worship culture founded by Abraham was not yet fully established in the family system. Abraham was a sojourner, but Isaac was a settler. Abraham had to keep on the move to feed his herds, but Isaac dug wells in order to settle and claim ownership of the land. Some nearby neighbors took offence and tried to take over these wells. As Isaac calmly permitted his wells to be used by others, God kept blessing him with new wells. Isaac's response resulted in personal prosperity and eventually, favor with his former antagonists. The supernatural increase of Isaac's livestock portfolio was undoubtedly provision for the next generation who would expand the family numbers dramatically. Most importantly, Isaac learned to hear the voice of God through which he received the same promise as his father.[60] He adopted his parents' value system and passed the inherited blessing on to the next generation. This is the primary task of the second generation and it's not always as easy as it looks.

Securing Both Ends of the Bridge

Half a bridge is no bridge at all. The battle to secure a bridge occurs at both ends. The second generation person must pay close attention to their

---

59   The details of Isaac's adult life can all be found in Genesis chapters 24 through 28

60   Genesis 26:24-25

connections with two very different generations: the one that came before and the one rising up after them. Let's see how this works.

Securing the Near End of the Bridge

I have witnessed many examples of second generation believers who fail to adopt their parent's faith. One of the issues for second generation believers is that they will never have the same life circumstances as their parents. And the second leader of an organization will never have the same stories to tell as the founder of that organization. Different generations will usually experience the same events from different perspectives. However, when they openly share their experience with each other, they can come to the same conclusions. Let's go back to the life of Isaac to see how this works.

In Genesis 22:1-19 God tested Abraham's faith by making what seems like a ridiculous request: 'sacrifice your only son on an altar'. Yet, it should be noted that many people *did do that* in Abraham's day in order to please their 'god'. It was the ultimate test of obeying God's voice. So Abraham and Isaac *journeyed together* with the wood, the fire and a knife. This story is usually called Abraham's sacrifice. *But how about giving Isaac some credit here?* I say this because Isaac wasn't a small child without options. Isaac was probably fifteen at the time, a young strong teenager who could have easily resisted the attempts of his centenarian father to tie him to a woodpile. If Isaac had said, '*No way old man. You are crazy! Hey everyone my dad has lost his marbles!*', then … end of story. But Isaac didn't bolt when the knife was raised. He had watched his dad in action long enough to know that God would show up! God told Abraham to stay his hand and a ram was provided, caught in a thicket, for the sacrifice. Father and son were experiencing this event in radically different ways, one about to have his life cut short, and the other about to lose a son of promise. However, as Abraham looked down on his son and Isaac looked up at his father, there was sacrifice and submission at both ends of the knife. Both father and son heard the voice of God who told Abraham to stay his hand. Both saw the ram caught in the bush. Walking back down that mountain, two different generations with different perspectives had come to the same conclusion: Trust God, no matter what, and He will provide. The 'front end' of the bridge (between the first and second generation) was now secured because father and son had walked together and shared the experience of God's testing and blessing upon their family.

Most children would not have submitted to the ropes that bound Isaac. Today, the children of those who have stepped out in faith will also battle the desire to break free from the parental storyline. Peer pressure encourages them to discard tradition in order to form a unique identity of their own making. In addition, the child who shares DNA with a great Pioneer may also, *by nature,* be a risk taker who wants to set out on their own great adventure. Author Paul Scanlon addresses this issue for second generation believers:

> "They want to be distinct and not just blend in with what their parents did, though they cannot deny that their parents' faith was awesome and has left them a great legacy. They want to establish their own faith and to be making their own choices, but they cannot get away from the truth that the best choices they can make are actually the same ones their parents made before them."[61]

This is why it is a great mistake to presume that the second generation will automatically adopt the beliefs and values of the first generation. Telling them what to believe is rarely sufficient. The winning way to secure the front end of the bridge is to *share authentic God-moments together* and to talk about them often as Deuteronomy chapter six tells us:

> "Impress them upon your children. Talk about them when you sit at home and when you walk along the road, when you lie down and when you get up."

Here is a testimony of how this worked for our own teen-aged daughter when she co-experienced our step of faith as Melissa and I pioneered a new ministry:

> "In my own house as a young adult, I saw my parents make a large leap of faith career wise into a vast unknown, grey misty future. They had just heard God's voice to leave pastoring. Big step. Would they obey? It meant no financial security. They would be putting their faith on the line in front of their blossoming young adult and teen children. Was God

---

61   *The Battle for the Loins* by Paul Scanlon, pg 88-89

real enough and loving enough to provide for our family? These moments are like busy traffic intersections with red lights, green lights, signs and people with their own opinions making their own choices. Even if you move ahead at a green light, there could be an accident! So my question was "Were my parents going to crash and burn if they tried to advance through this intersection? Or would God show up?"

We watched as my parents moved forward. It would happen that they would need a specific amount of money that month. They would cry out to God reminding Him of His promises and His words. They would read His word, pray, worship, praise and be thankful. And that week they would receive the amount needed to cover the bills. We watched this happen time after time, year after year. Every single time, God provided. I never went hungry. I never went without clothes or friends or blessings. *The truth that it was God making all this possible was rooted in my soul.* Today I am grown up and have my own family. To this day I do not worry about finances. My marriage has been free of financial stress and worry, because it was instilled in me from the generations before me that I am loved and protected for by Jehovah Jireh, My Provider. A baton was passed to me of rock-solid trust in a God who will always provide not only finances but whatever I need. I will never be abandoned."

Another challenge that may present itself to the second generation believers is the reputation of their parents. Those who grow up in the shadow of pioneering parents may feel like they will never measure up to what they have witnessed. The shining example of their parents can unintentionally set the bar of success impossibly high. Therefore, Pioneer Parents need to make sure they understand who their children are *in God's eyes* and mentor them in becoming *that person*, not a copy of themselves.

Franklin Graham grew up always being identified as the son of legendary Evangelist Billy Graham. Billy, by his own confession, was away from home too often for the good of his children when they were in their formative years. Franklin wanted to establish his own identity and, by *his* own confession, took the long road to embracing his true identity as the Next Gen Leader of a world-shaping ministry. Once that was settled, Franklin not only assumed the leadership of the Billy Graham Evangelistic Association, he also founded Samaritan's Purse, one of the largest humanitarian organizations in the U.S. I once traveled as a chaplain with a Samaritan's Purse group to South America and I saw firsthand the incredible cultural penetration this ministry was providing for the Gospel. Franklin will never preach to as many people face to face as his father did. Yet it seems to me that, through Samaritan's Purse, the impact of Franklin's ministry may eventually extend beyond that of his famous father.

Securing the Far End of the Bridge

Let's look at what it takes to secure the far end of the bridge. We begin with some graphic examples of how easy it is to neglect this link between the second and third generations.

<blockquote>

Joshua neglected to do for the next generation what had been done for him.

</blockquote>

Moses was a great pioneer leader. Joshua began as Moses' personal assistant[62] and was groomed for many years to become the next national leader. The transfer of spiritual and governmental authority from Moses to Joshua was well planned and accompanied by great ceremony.[63] Joshua became a conquering hero. *Yet Joshua apparently neglected to do for the next generation what had been done for him.* In contrast to Moses, there is no record of Joshua mentoring any future leader. Joshua's final discourse to the nation contains no commissioning or ceremonial transfer. He gives warnings without blessings. Joshua concludes with some rather critical comments of his followers followed by an abrupt dismissal.[64] Consequently, the Bible records that once Joshua and his peers had died, *"another generation grew up who knew neither the Lord nor what He had done for Israel."*[65]

---

62   Exodus 24:13

63   Numbers 27:18-19

64   Joshua chapter 24 - especially verses 19 and 28

65   Judges 2:10

It's pretty well the same story with Elijah and Elisha. Elijah mentored his protegé Elisha with father-like care. Elisha asked for and received an even greater anointing for prophecy and miracles. But when he died there was no one standing there crying 'my father, my father!' as Elisha had done when Elijah passed. There was no living person prepared to carry Elisha's anointing. It rested with his dead bones[66].

You see the same thing happening today. Often, second generation children have not shared in the lean years of sacrifice experienced by the Pioneer generation. They have only experienced the fruit of that sacrifice in the form of great favor and blessing. *Having grown up seeing nothing but success it's easy to assume that convoy of blessing will automatically 'keep on rolling'.* As Joshua and Elisha demonstrated, nothing could be further from the truth.

Every generation needs to build a bridge to connect the former ways to the future days. But the second generation is the *first generation* of many to do so. Second generation believers and organizational leaders must never forget all that went into making them the person they have become. *They must 'go and do likewise' by making sure they invest a commensurate amount of time and energy into preparing the next generation.* They must distill the unrefined experiences from the previous generation into a transferable lifestyle for future generations.

Remember, half a bridge is no bridge at all. Second Generation Leaders, fulfilment of the visions of the Pioneer Generation depend upon you securing both ends of the bridge. Don't allow their hard-earned victories to be relegated to the bookshelves of history. Keep the story alive as you follow God's voice in every decision. Like Isaac, you can expect to receive a level of supernatural increase that will become provision for many generations to come.

---

66   2 Kings 13:20-21

CHAPTER 8

The Occupier Generation

Sow a thought, reap an action.
Sow an action, reap a habit.
Sow a habit, reap a character.
Sow a character, reap a destiny.
Ralph Waldo Emerson

Sow a destiny, reap a dynasty
Terry Bone

O ne day while planning a trip to Israel with Yaffa, my Israeli travel agent, I asked her "*Where do you come from?*" To me that question meant, in which city were you born? I was thinking maybe Tel Aviv or Haifa. To Yaffa that question meant something entirely different. Staring at me as if I had just landed from outer space, she exclaimed, "*What? You are a Pastor of the Bible and you do not know where I come from? Why, I come from Abraham of course!*"

Now, that's generational thinking! Yaffa went on to explain that she had traced her immediate family roots back as far as the Babylonian Captivity![67] Then, matter of factly, she added, "*our family didn't go with the captives, we stayed in the Holy Land during the entire seventy years*". For a moment I thought she was kidding me. Apparently not. This sense of identity rooted in a hundred generations of history is *normal* for Yaffa and many of her fellow descendants of Abraham. In spite of multiple periods of persecution and exile over the centuries, the Jews have returned to their land, their language and ultimately will return to their Lord. Now that's permanence!

Momentum
At what point does an inter-generational blessing, business or ministry become so well ingrained that it generates a virtually permanent momentum? I

---

67   The Jewish tribe of Judah was captured and taken to Babylon in approximately 600 B.C. Yaffa was therefore claiming to know her family's history for over 2,500 years!

believe the *third generation* represents the potential tipping point. For the first generation, the ways of God are countercultural. They move in the opposite direction to the generational pattern. Each subsequent generation that chooses to continue in the ways of the first generation, creates a little more momentum. By the third generation, the family values are strong and well defined.

For the second generation it is optional and for the third it is normal.

A third generation believer often has the direct influence of godly parents *and* grandparents.

You could say that for the first generation the choice is *exceptional;* for the second generation it is *optional* and for the third it is *normal.* You can call it spiritual momentum. While it does not violate the gift of free choice granted to every human being, it is experienced as a constant current, nudging the third generation believer towards God's grace and favor. Paul Scanlon describes it this way:

> "That momentum is actually a gift to the third generation from the former two; it sweeps over them, urging them forward to perpetuate the line of faith. Momentum is the power of the movement. The third generation are born into it and it is an incredible gift and positive asset if they can see it this way."[68]

Jacob experienced it. He grew up in a family that honored God with sacrifice. The altar was central, the voice of God was frequent and blessing was expected. His father Isaac had pronounced that Jacob would be the one to actually *possess* the promises his grandfather had only seen by faith:

---

68 *The Battle for the Loins* (Abundant Life Publishing West Yorkshire UK), page 134,

"May [the Lord] give you and your descendants the blessing given to Abraham so that you may take possession of the land."[69]

This blessing was confirmed with an unprecedented dream that God would 'open Heaven' over his family and descendants represented by the angels ascending and descending on a stairway [or ladder].[70]

Ownership

So, what is the battle for this generation? First it's about taking ownership. Isaac's blessing for Jacob included the phrase '*that you may take possession*'. Jacob was in a battle to *receive* what Abraham had *believed*. It took a while for Jacob to understand that. As Paul Scanlon says, the momentum received by the third generation is a positive asset '*if they can see it this way*'. At first Jacob *didn't* see it that way because he was still engaged in two other battles: to do things his own way and to overcome inherited family patterns that were ungodly. Strong-willed Jacob wanted to inherit the land and the family blessing, but he wanted to do it *on his own terms*.

It seems to me that one of the reasons for Jacob's self-will was that he had not experienced the faithfulness of God *for himself* in the same manner as Abraham and Isaac had. Until he left home, Jacob hadn't needed to trust God for much. Everything was provided for him. So, at the outset of his journey from Canaan, Jacob was not yet at that place of personal relationship with God demonstrated by his forefathers. When God appeared to him at Bethel, Jacob didn't say 'How awesome is this God!' He said 'How awesome is this place!'.[71] He probably thought he had lucked out by choosing to sleep near some holy location. Jacob then makes a vow to serve God back in this location *if* God will be with him. Yet moments before, God had promised Jacob that very thing![72] In my viewpoint, Jacob missed an opportunity to take the short path to permanence on this occasion because he was not yet living in the awareness of the covenantal love of his God. Consequently, he embarked on a *twenty year* journey of discovering the faithfulness of God. The journey was completed on the night that Jacob wrestled with an 'angel'

---

69   Genesis 28:4

70   Genesis 28:10-15

71   A paraphrase of Genesis 28:16

72   Compare Genesis 28:15 with 28:20

and finally took ownership of the covenantal promise passed down from his grandfather.[73] After that event, Jacob returned to Canaan with a new name reflecting his spiritual victories.[74]

Overcoming Family Patterns

Remember what God told Moses on the mountain? The sins of the fathers continue for three and four generations. It's that phenomenon that third generation believers have to deal with in a greater way than those before them. Everyone commits their own sins. Everyone has 'their own stuff' that they need to overcome. Sins not dealt with in one generation, add to each generation's struggles. They pass along a momentum that nudges following generations in the wrong direction. However, it doesn't always show up as a serious problem *until the third generation*.

It reminds me of the peach tree in our backyard. Our tree has a 'years to fruit' rating of three, meaning that it takes three years from transplantation to visible fruit. The first year we planted that little stick in our yard, it looked like nothing was happening. In fact you couldn't see much difference between that tree and the Maple sapling on the other side of the fence. The second year there were buds and leaves. Not until the third year did the fruit appear. Only then was it obvious that we had a peach tree in our yard. It can be the same with sinful generational patterns which reside in the heart of the first generation and appear to be doing little harm. However, if these habits are left unchecked, then by the third generation *we will have a visible problem*. The characteristic battle of the third generation is to weed out those patterns, forsake those familiar habits and pave the way for permanence with personal purity.

This dynamic is clearly evident in the story of Abraham's family. Abraham was a man full of faith and righteous in all his ways - *almost*. He told a lie. Just a little one. Some might call it a 'white lie', an untruth told for a good cause.[75] At the time, Abraham was camping out at Bethel in the promised land. Due to famine, Abraham leaves the place of blessing and takes his

---

73   Genesis chapter 32

74   Jacob means 'one who takes the place of another' and Israel, his new name, means one who has striven with God and prevailed.'

75   The whole story is found in Genesis 12:10-20

family to Egypt. There's no record that Abraham heard God's voice in this decision - perhaps he was following the voice of fear. As Abraham and Sarah entered Egypt, Abraham voices his fear of being harmed because of his wife's beauty. In order to protect himself, he asks her to lie and say she is his sister. Evidently, he wasn't thinking much about the consequences for Sarah! The plan backfired when the Pharaoh took Sarah to become a concubine.[76] Years later, the Bible records that Isaac did *precisely the same thing* with his wife Rebekah and not surprisingly ran into the same problem![77] As they say, 'like father, like son'.

The battle for purity in the third generation can prove to be the deciding factor.

By the third generation this little 'white lie' habit grew to become a full blown family pattern of deception. Jacob and his mother plotted to deceive Isaac into giving Jacob the special firstborn family blessing that they were afraid would be wasted on an unspiritual Esau. That did not work out well. It caused the family to split up for decades. Jacob ran from his brother's threats but the pattern of deception tagged along with him. Uncle Laban later pulled the same identity theft trick on Jacob that Jacob had tried to pull on his own father, by switching one sister for the other on Jacob's wedding night! What was permitted in moderation by the first and second generations had landed upon the third generation with force. For the next twenty years, Jacob's life was a mixture of blessing and trouble until it was finally settled during the overnight wrestling match with the mysterious Heavenly being. In that famous encounter, Jacob was in a battle for purity. He was allowing God to deal with the *fruit* of sinful patterns by pulling out the *root*.

The battle for purity in the third generation can prove to be the deciding factor in creating a permanent possession of the promise. The more that the first and second generation deal with their character issues, the less they will leave for the third generation to contend with, and the more likely the battle for permanence will be won. Whenever the third generation *does* win the

---

76   I am guessing this represented a low point in Abe and Sarah's emotional intimacy.

77   Compare Genesis 20 with Genesis 26:1-11

battle for purity, then the enemy's attempts to block the intergenerational flow of blessing is outflanked. Jacob won his family battle and the right to be named along with dad and granddad in God's favorite title '*the God of Abraham, Isaac and Jacob*'. (He also acquired a new name, Israel - meaning 'one who has prevailed') *Now* Jacob was ready to raise up that world shaper of a boy named Joseph.

> The most dedicated followers
> of Jesus among us are still
> subject to negative family
> patterns at some level.

Everyone's Battle

The most dedicated followers of Jesus among us are still subject to negative family patterns at some level. I have watched this generational dynamic play out in so many lives that it has become easy to spot in a conversation. For example, any time the answer to an important question about behavior is "That's the way we've always done it", a little warning light goes off on the dashboard of my mind that says "*caution, generational patterns ahead*". Even when they seem to be minor, sooner or later, they will surface in the form of harmful behavior. The best news in all of this is that Jacob's private struggle became a public victory and paved the way for his son Joseph to change the course of a nation. It also kept the promises flowing to countless generations to follow.

With that in mind, every leader, every parent and anyone walking in the blessing of preceding generations ought to remember that *there is no such thing as minor obedience*. Reaping always follows sowing. And we always reap *more* than we sow. Your personal obedience will become the next generation's corporate inheritance.

PART THREE
The Exchange Zone

———

The Exchange Zone is a track and field term for the marked area in a lane of track where two relay runners must meet and exchange the baton. This part of the book deals exclusively with the 'what to do' and the 'how to do it' in that zone. These are principles that span all applications of passing the baton between two generations, including the batons of faith, of leadership, and also the business world.

Using the word B-A-T-O-N as an acrostic, a chapter is devoted to each letter describing the necessary elements for success:

B is for BAG Chapter 9

We all have some amount of emotional baggage. This chapter will give an overview of what's typically in that bag and how to set it down.

A is for ANOINTING Chapter 10

Anointing is defined as the unique blend of *Spiritual authority and ability* that each of us carries as followers of Jesus Christ. This chapter will discuss how to understand what you carry and how to bestow it upon the next generation.

T is for TIMING Chapter 11

Getting the timing of transitions right is always crucial. This chapter discusses how to not miss the moment by investing in the right people at the right time and learning to discern the voice of God in the process.

O is for OTHER-CENTERED Chapter 12

Other-centered behavior is simple to understand yet eludes our grasp all too often. This chapter examines the profound generational consequences that follow a lack of prioritizing those who follow after us.

N *is for NEXT* Chapter 13

Our minds and hearts must be pointed in the direction where God is going, not where we have been. *This chapter examines how to identify the NEXT thing and the NEXT person that God has in store* for the race in which you have been placed. The role of the Holy Spirit is essential as no one can get this right using human logic alone.

CHAPTER 9

Drop the Bag!

————

We teach what we know, but we reproduce who we are.
John Maxwell

You Won't Need That Here

The morning after my father-in-law died, I had a brief but vivid dream through which God spoke a message to me that I will never forget. In order for you to feel the impact of this message to my heart, I will provide a brief backstory.

My father-in-law, Dick Wukasch, died suddenly in his 92nd year due to a fall while out shopping. At that time he had been an ordained Lutheran Minister for more than 60 years (in the USA and Canada). Having been raised during the Great Depression of the 1930s he and his wife Sylvia raised six children on a meager salary, regularly stretching a dollar in ways we can't imagine today. Dick and Sylvia made it a priority to live their faith openly before their children and taught them how to live according to biblical principles.

Dick had grown up in tough times and his frequent storytelling revealed glimpses into a difficult childhood. Dick had suffered significant emotional pain, but like most men of his generation, he didn't know where to park that pain. The family and church culture of his day did not allow for such discussions. Young people were told 'time heals everything', and 'someone has it worse than you'. They were admonished to 'just read your Bible and do the right thing.' And so although Rev. Dick Wukasch was a decent father and man of faith, he also carried what is often called 'emotional baggage'. A few hours after Dick had been swiftly ushered into the presence of his Savior, I had the following dream:

> I was inside a passenger train which was stopped at a station. I was looking through a large window at my father-in-law who was standing on the platform. In my dream I understood that he had just exited the train because this was his station but it was not my station. He was dressed in a black cap and overcoat and he was holding a black duffel bag. Although he

was facing away from me, I could tell that he was looking to see who would greet him. Then I heard a disembodied voice speak to him. It was the kindest voice you could imagine. I could feel the emotion and the love as this voice welcomed Dick. Regarding his duffel bag, the voice said with a light chuckle, "You can set that down, you *won't need that here*".

Immediately I awoke and felt like I was being bathed in "liquid love". This was obviously the Heavenly Father's voice welcoming Dick at his final stop in life! Even the fact that the setting was a train station was significant as my father-in-law loved to travel by train. What I remember most vividly is the *kindness* and the gentle manner in which the Heavenly voice spoke to my father-in-law. Next to that voice, the most striking thing about the dream was *the Heavenly Father's response to the duffel bag*. Somehow I knew that the bag was a metaphor for all the things that Dick liked to hold onto to make himself feel secure. In essence God was saying that when we arrive in Heaven, we will finally, once and for all, leave behind all our unresolved issues. There will be no trace of the emotional and mental baggage we have carried around so long we barely notice its weight when things are going smoothly.

No one wins a race
carrying a suitcase.

At once this dream pointed my heart in two directions. On the one hand, it brought peace and release to me regarding my father-in-law. Any unresolved issue from his painful past had been set down and left behind. Now he could extend both his arms in a loving embrace with his true Father. At the same time, the dream shone a light into my own heart. There was an extraordinary clarity about how senseless it is to carry emotional baggage for an entire lifetime. After all, no one wins a race carrying a suitcase.

What's in the Bag?

Imagine trying to run a race while you're holding a large bag full of extra equipment. It's going to slow you down. Imagine an Olympic runner stopping on the track to open up and look inside a bag for the baton. Other runners smoothly slip past him while his teammate waits. It's unthinkable in an actual track event, but it's not too far off what happens in real life.

There are two categories of things in that bag which slow us down according to the letter to Hebrews which says, "Therefore, since we are surrounded by such a huge crowd of witnesses to the life of faith, *let us strip off every <u>weight</u> that slows us down, and the <u>sin</u> that so easily trips us up.*" [78]

Anything that doesn't help you run the race is something that hinders your race.

Sinful behavior is one of the weighty items in that bag we carry, especially when we try to conceal it from others' view. Sinful habits weigh us down and cause us to stumble outside of the lanes of God's Commandments. No matter how much we try to ignore it, conceal it or minimize its impact, sin that remains unconfessed will seriously slow us down and may even cause us to become disqualified from the race.[79] Hidden sin also acts like a unseen virus in our soul which is easily passed on to the next generation. Enough said.

On the other hand, the phrase '*every weight that slows us down*' requires a little more explanation. These weights are not sins per se, but rather any belief or behavior we hold on to that works against our success. Let me put it this way: *anything that doesn't help you run the race is something that hinders your race.*

The list of hindrances is long. It includes all sorts of behaviors that distract us or discourage us. They are not too hard to spot in others, and if our heart is teachable then our own can also be identified. What is less visible are the beliefs that drive our behaviors. *That's what's inside the bag.* While this list is also not exactly short, I want to focus on what I consider the big three: *faulty church doctrines, faulty cultural beliefs and faulty character.*

Faulty Church Doctrine

---

78   Hebrews 12:1 NLT (New Living Translation) The NIV translates 'every weight that slows us down' as 'everything that hinders.'

79   At least temporarily. I want the reader to understand that there is always forgiveness extended by the Grace of God no matter how long we have wandered from the truth.

I have intentionally chosen to use the word 'faulty' rather than 'false'. Some doctrines are blatantly false and heretical, such as the teaching that Jesus is a created being on the same order as the angels. I am not dealing with that kind here. By faulty, I am referring to the doctrinal emphases that, though they have elements of truth in them, push too hard in one direction. In so doing, they capture our emotions and lead us astray. Here are a couple of prime examples:

The first is the very popular half-truth that God wants to make us all wealthy in this life, the so-called 'Prosperity Gospel'. Now don't get me wrong, I like prosperity. I tried being poor and it didn't make me happy at all. And Proverbs tells us that a wise person accumulates wealth for their children's children.[80] It's not the wealth per se, it's the focus of our attention. I agree with the preacher David Wilkerson who said that too often we spend our faith on *ourselves*. Spending my faith to acquire stuff that's all going to burn is *not* generational thinking. Too much focus upon my own material prosperity, no matter how spiritual it sounds, will fog over the windshield of my spiritual vision. I will be in danger of losing sight of what I am supposed to be passing on to the next generation and missing the Exchange Zone altogether.

Another faulty doctrine is the hyper-faith message which asserts that if you have enough faith, then you will get what you ask for *every time*. Inevitably, no matter how full of faith a person is, they will not *always* get exactly what they ask for in a specific situation. When that happens, someone must be blamed. False guilt and shame circle this kind of belief like vultures waiting to land on the one who 'fails'. I know of a pastor who was renowned for his faith. He preached that if you have enough faith you will be healed every time you ask. He died of cancer in his late fifties. Many in his congregation would not attend the funeral of their own pastor as they assumed he was somehow to blame for his own lack of healing.

Other doctrines in the 'faulty' category include the kind of legalism that teaches that certain sins disqualify a person from full restoration even after repentance. At the other extreme we find the 'hyper-grace' doctrine that masquerades as God's love but in reality teaches that you can sin all you want and at the same time enjoy uninterrupted fellowship with God. Whole

---

80   Proverbs 13:22

books have been written about each of the faulty doctrines mentioned above. All I am saying here is that these kinds of faulty beliefs will eventually bear bad fruit in our hearts. They will add emotional baggage that weighs us down and hinders us from running the good race that God has set before us.

Faulty Church Culture

Another weight is our constant tendency to treat the rules of church culture like they were Biblical commands. In Jesus' day the Pharisees created 613 laws for people to follow. Yet Jesus told His followers that you could boil the entire law down to the first two Commandments;

> Love God with all your heart, mind and soul
> Love your neighbour as yourself.[81]

Today we also are fond of adding rules that have little or nothing to do with the actual Gospel. They complicate the message, and add unnecessary weight for the next runner. When I was considering which example to use to illustrate this, the voices in my head were many. So just for fun, I decided to pick an extreme case to make the point.

In the early 1990's I was asked to be a conference speaker in a country where our denomination was doing missions work among a very isolated and remote indigenous people. The local missionaries had successfully brought the Gospel to these people. It seems they also brought *church culture* to them. For example, anyone assigned to teach or preach from the pulpit had to wear a tie (like we wear with a business suit). It was such a strict rule that a call to ministry was referred to by locals as '*a call to the tie*'. The ludicrous part of this story is that the locals actually *didn't wear any clothes* most of the time. These particular locals were accustomed to the Adam and Eve look, with or without the fig leaf. This gave the phrase 'dressing up for church' a whole new meaning. Some did put on western clothes, while others preferred to attend church clothed only with 'power from on high'. But rules are rules, so a tie was still mandatory in order to speak from the pulpit. (My trip ended up being cancelled but I had prepared myself by purchasing a *really long* tie.) Back here in North America, some of our church rules make no more sense than wearing only a tie to church! They simply add unnecessary baggage,

---

81   Mark 12:29-30

especially when we adopt them into our belief system and make the race far more complicated than was ever intended.

Once again you can add as many items as you want to this list.

Faulty Character

Faulty character includes all forms of emotional immaturity, such as unforgiveness, competitiveness, a quick temper and the need to be the center of attention. Individual sins will never disqualify us if they are confessed and forsaken. But when these behaviors are chronic, they become part of our character, weighing us down as we run our race. Emotional immaturity is a big deal. *You cannot be spiritually mature if you remain emotionally immature.*[82] Think of how this plays out when it comes to passing the baton. If a leader is emotionally insecure - holding on to their position to prop up a weak sense of identity - then he or she may be reluctant to groom a young leader who looks as if they may have superior talents. That's a loss for the whole team. In addition, certain emotional attributes are particularly transferable. When a leader arrives in the Exchange Zone with anger or fear, there may be a baton to pass but it's *inside* an emotional bag which is hard to handle.

With respect to families, the same principle applies. The most dedicated parents who employ the most sophisticated methods for parenting still have trouble passing the baton of faith if they are fear driven or carry anger. Their children may not be willing or able to sort through that bag and fish out the baton. The best thing a parent can do for their child is to discard their own emotional baggage. It starts with becoming excellent at giving and receiving forgiveness, and continues by learning to replace embedded lies from past hurts with the present truth of the Father's love.

When God reveals it,
He heals it.

Let me press in a little more on this crucial point. Denial is not the same as freedom. You cannot forsake something you cannot see. In the same

---

82   Peter and Geri Scazzero first coined this phrase. They offer life-changing resources at emotionallyhealthy.org

passage that Paul says he forsakes what lies behind, he also says that we all should have mature attitudes and if not *the Lord will reveal it to us*.[83] When God reveals it, He heals it. Through God's Word, prayer, counseling and encounters with the Holy Spirit, the lies and pain can be revealed, erased and replaced with God's truth. False guilt and shame which paralyze our ability to run our race, can be overcome in the same manner. Then, mom and dad, the precious baton you carry will be in plain view, reflecting the light of God's glory.

If you are sensing that you need some help in this area, I want to encourage you that the most important factor in beginning the process of transformation is courage. It takes courage to stop the momentum of your daily life for a brief season and get some assistance to open up and sort through that bag. It's not pleasant to be reminded of such things. Just remember that the *prize* is always worth the *price*. The brief discomfort you endure will pay huge dividends for you and especially for those waiting in the Exchange Zone to take hold of the *good things* that you carry. Don't hand them a bag, give them a baton.

---

83   Philippians 3:13-15

CHAPTER 10

Know Your Anointing

You can receive something you don't understand, but you cannot transfer something you don't understand.

Pastor Bill Johnson, Redding CA

The name 'Jesus Christ' means 'Jesus the Anointed One'.[84] Jesus began His ministry by announcing and describing the anointing given to Him;

> "The Spirit of the Lord is on me because He has *anointed* me..."[85]

Jesus understood the anointing He carried and how it enabled Him to bring the Kingdom of Heaven to Earth.

As a follower of Jesus Christ, you also have an anointing.[86] He gave it to you. You carry it with you. It too has the potential to bring Heaven's power and presence to earth. Your anointing is similar in nature to other followers of Jesus yet uniquely blended for your specific life calling. It's yours to use for God's glory under the direction of the Holy Spirit. *You also have the right and the responsibility to pass on your anointing to others over the course of your life and ministry.*

As a follower of Jesus Christ, you have an anointing.

There is a profound lack of clarity on this topic of 'anointing' among many Christians. A lot of people I know use this word to describe the sensation

---

84 The word 'Christ' comes from the Greek **word** *Christos,* **meaning** 'anointed one'

85 Luke 4:18-21

86 *"... you have an anointing from the Holy One, and all of you know the truth ..."* 1 John 2:20

of feeling God's presence: "*Wow, that was an anointed service. I really felt the Holy Spirit's presence*," or "*That sermon was anointed, I could feel the power of God*". The feelings associated with the manifest presence of God are not what the Bible refers to as the anointing. The Biblical definition can be summarized as *the Spiritual authority and ability to bring the Kingdom of Heaven to earth.*[87] The Godly use of that authority often produces the manifest presence of the Holy Spirit, but to think of the presence itself as the actual anointing is to miss the mark.

A Quick Study on the Anointing

According to British tradition, the transfer of regal authority must include a ceremony in which the regent is anointed with oil. They are inseparable. At the Coronation of Queen Elizabeth II, the Archbishop of Canterbury uttered these words as he anointed the new Queen with oil:

> "*Be thy head anointed with holy oil, as kings, priests, and prophets were anointed.*
>
> And as Solomon was anointed king by Zadok the priest and Nathan the prophet, *so be you anointed, blessed and consecrated...to rule and govern*"[88]

The Archbishop was referring to the Old Testament practice in which a concoction of oil and perfume was smeared upon people appointed to positions of authority, mainly prophets, priests and kings.[89] These recipes were deliberately designed to give off a strong and pleasant fragrance as a symbol of the newly-resident authority upon that person. But once the fragrance and the physical oil had worn off, *the position of authority remained.*

---

87   This is my sound-bite version of what the Bible reveals through the combined revelation of the Old and New Testament references to anointing. The Old Testament symbolizes what the Gospels clearly define on this topic. Central to this definition are three things: First the title Christ means anointed one. Secondly, Luke 4:16-20 was Jesus' self-proclaimed definition of His earthly ministry. Thirdly, His recorded words (John 14:12) made it clear that we are to do the same works.

88   Taken from the online article at https://www.bbc.com/news/uk-22764987 accessed July 2018

89   Some examples are found in Exodus 29:7, 30:22-25, 37:29, 40:15

How can you give away something you don't know you have?

In the New Testament, the anointing is the *authority and ability* given to every believer to operate in the power of the Holy Spirit to bring the Kingdom of Heaven to earth.[90] This authority is often accompanied by the Spiritual 'fragrance' of God's manifest presence, something we can feel or sense in a tangible way. However, the fragrance, or sense of presence, is not the anointing. The anointing is *the authority and the ability* that it represents. The feelings associated with the presence of the Holy Spirit may come and go, but the anointing He has given to every believer remains. The Apostle John explicitly tells us so:

> *"As for you, the anointing you received from him remains in you... as his anointing teaches you about all things and as that anointing is real, not counterfeit—just as it has taught you, remain in him."* (emphasis mine) 1 John 2:27

How can you give away something you don't know you have? Even if you do believe you have some level of Spiritual authority, *if you can't define it, how can you be sure you have actually passed it on?* So, let's start by defining the word 'authority'.

Anointing Represents Authority

Authority is *the right to use power*. Authority must be given by someone who already possesses an equal or higher level of that same authority. When a politician, judge or government official is sworn in, they are *given* certain levels of authority bestowed upon them on behalf of the entire government. The invisible power they carry is real. The laws they make, interpret and enforce can change your life in profound ways. Likewise, the invisible authority of the anointing you carry is also real. It also can change the lives around you in profound ways. Your God-given authority is part of the package of redemption. Adam and Eve were originally given a high level of authority, the right to rule over the entire earth (Genesis 1:28). The devil

---

90   Luke 4:18 again. Whatever is true of Jesus as an anointed man, is true for all followers of Jesus based upon His own words in John 14:12

usurped this authority from them by leading them into sin[91]. Jesus won back that right to rule. He bought it back at the cost of His own life. That's why He announced after His resurrection that "*All Authority under Heaven and earth has been given to me.*"[92]

Jesus not only modeled an anointed life to perfection, He also announced that anyone who believes could do the same things He had been doing.[93] In other words, *He was intending to share His anointing with every single one of his followers.* Every follower of Jesus shares certain aspects of Christ's delegated authority with other followers, such as the indwelling Holy Spirit and the ability to overcome the power of sin in our lives. In addition, each of us has a unique blend of Spiritual gifts and natural talents which are also invested with Heavenly authority. As a result, there will be certain people, places and situations where the exercise of your gifts bring extraordinary results. *The anointing that rests upon your life releases the operation of that inherent authority.* The anointing becomes visibly evident when people are impacted by your words or defer to your wisdom. It is also seen through direct answers to your prayers and the power of the Spirit released through the exercise of your gifts. And because it resides in you as a gift from God, you have the responsibility to steward this anointing. You also have the right to transfer it to those who follow after you.

Know What You Carry

We have arrived at the core of what it means to carry a baton of faith and pass it on. We are going beyond the typical talk about living your life as an inspiring example. This is more than legacy, this is potency! My first Pastor, George Tunks, understood the potency of what was entrusted to him through the Holy Spirit. As I mentioned in the opening chapter, God had placed upon his life an authority when it came to exercising and imparting the gifts of

---

91   Genesis 1:28 records the original mandate for people to administer God's authoritative rule over the entire earth. This right was forfeited through disobedience to God's command. Satan (the devil) usurped Adam and Eve's authority until a person could win it back through perfect sinless obedience. Jesus did so. That is why Jesus is referred to as 'the second Adam' in the book of Romans.

92   Matthew 28:18

93   In John 14:12-14 and Matthew 28:18-20 Jesus declares that we have been given shared authority of both His *words* and His *works*

the Holy Spirit. Gifts of healing, faith and miracles were regular occurrences in his ministry. Back then there was a popular notion that a person needed to log an inordinate number of hours 'seeking God' or 'praying through' at the altar before they qualified for certain Spiritual gifts[94]. Pastor George believed that Jesus already paid the price for our gifts, and would grant gifts to those who asked in faith. Like the Apostle Paul who laid his hands upon Timothy to impart Spiritual gifts, George would lay his hands on any sincere person who came forward and more often than not the results would be evident within a few moments. George Tunks had an evident authority in this area, an anointing, that lifted others' faith level to match his own. His ministry approach cut across the grain of unbelief expressed in the traditions of his day. Decades before the existence of cell phones with cameras, reports leaked out about the remarkable results occurring in his meetings. A high-ranking Church official showed up at a meeting to see for himself what exactly was going on. This man of God walked along behind George observing everything he did. The results were immediate and obvious. After the meeting he exclaimed, "Well I have to change what I believe about this. God *can* give His gifts without delay!"

Anointing is not limited to teaching or preaching.

The anointing resting upon Pastor George changed the minds and altered the practices of denominational leaders. They deferred to the anointing resting upon his life. When *you* understand the extent and nature of your particular Spiritual giftedness, then you will also have exceptional success in that area. You will have a high level of expectation and perform well without a struggle. People will tend to defer to you in that area.

Anointing is not limited to teaching or preaching. Some, like mastercraftsman Bezalel have also been "filled with the Spirit of God, with skill, ability and

---

94   This was especially true for the so-called Baptism of the Holy Spirit and the gift of tongues. 'Tarrying' meetings were common practice. These consisted of prayer meetings that were many hours or even days long, held for the purpose of waiting for the moment that God would bestow His gifts upon the seekers.

knowledge in all kinds of crafts".[95] He was an anointed construction worker! That reminds me of a mission trip I led consisting of two large teams, one dedicated to prayer and the other to construction. One of the team members, who was not designated as a leader, possessed a combination of knowledge and composure that led to the entire team deferring to him in all aspects of construction. He was a 'Bezalel', anointed for this kind of role. It was interesting to see how people were drawn far more to this anointed person rather than to the one with the title.

It's easy to become distracted by the daily grind of making a living and providing for those who depend on us. Or perhaps we have become discouraged by an apparent lack of results. During those times, we must never lose sight of the anointing that God has entrusted to us. During a difficult period of time when Elijah was heavily burdened with the spiritual welfare of the nation, God made it clear that it was time to transfer his anointing to three other persons.[96] Elijah didn't respond by saying 'How do I do that?' He understood what he carried and, apparently, how to pass it along. With renewed energy, Elijah immediately left the place of prayer and anointed those who God had called to the task.

How Anointing is Transferred

Pieced together, the snippets of narrative about Elijah and Elisha, Paul the Apostle and the life of Jesus provide a picture of what it takes to transfer the anointing from one life to another. I am going to sum it up in three words: Revelation, Education and Impartation.

Revelation

Sometimes it is easy to understand who should receive the baton pass. If you are a parent, then the answer is obvious - your children, whether they be biological, adopted or fostered. In most other applications, the leading of the Holy Spirit is required to accurately identify those whom God has made ready and qualified to receive what you have to give. Elijah was confused

---

95   Exodus 31:3

96   *"Anoint Hazael king over Aram. Also, anoint Jehu son of Nimshi king over Israel, and anoint Elisha son of Shaphat from Abel Meholah to succeed you as prophet."* 1 Kings 19:15-16 NIV

until *God revealed* that what Elijah was carrying would be multiplied into the lives of King Hazael, Jehu and the prophet Elisha. It doesn't have to come exactly like that. Sometimes a combination of both observation and revelation brings the answer. The important point here is to ask God to show you and then wait for Him to reveal it in the manner and the timing He chooses.

Education

There is a very human element to this whole idea of passing along spiritual anointing. Elijah's transfer began with a direct revelation from God about Elisha. However, he followed it up with a period of mentorship and training. Elisha served as Elijah's personal assistant and budding prophet for perhaps six to eight years.[97] Elisha was known as the one who "poured water on the hands of Elijah."[98] Likewise, Jesus passed his anointing to his disciples through the gift of the Holy Spirit, but they also hung out with him for three years in a sort of first century version of a university co-op program combining academic and work experience!

And parents take note: The gold standard for transferring family blessing to the next generation is revealed in Moses' final instructions to the family clans of Israel: *"These commandments that I give you today are to be on your hearts. Impress them on your children. Talk about them when you sit at home and when you walk along the road, when you lie down and when you get up. Tie them as symbols on your hands and bind them on your foreheads. Write them on the doorframes of your houses and on your gates."*[99] Starting in your own home, teach and model the qualities you want to see transferred to those who are compatible with your calling and passion in life.

Impartation

In the Old Testament, anointing was accompanied by ceremony and symbols.[100] In New Testament times we have retained the practice of using actual

---

97   This approximation is derived from the timeline of the kings of Judah and Israel during the narrative of these two prophets lives.

98   2 Kings 3:11

99   Deuteronomy 6:6-9 NIV

100   In 1 Kings 19:19 we have the story of Elijah placing his cloak (or mantle) on Elisha as a symbol of the transfer of anointing. This term has been adopted into the language of certain church sub-cultures where you may hear talk of placing or transferring a

oil and the laying on of hands. The oil used is merely a symbol of the Holy Spirit, but the laying on of hands is more than symbolic. It is one of the means of transfer of Spiritual gifts and presence. From his prison cell, the Apostle Paul wrote to Timothy; *"I remind you to fan into flames the gift of God, which is in you through the laying on of my hands."*[101] I believe that we ought to go beyond the typical use of the laying on of hands for things such as ordination ceremonies. What you carry *can* be imparted. When you have the right person in front of you at the right time, God will honor the act with a tangible infusion of presence and power for one who receives in faith.

Pass It On

The anointing you carry now will be of no use to you in Heaven. You won't need to bring God's presence and power to anyone around you - they will already be filled with the Glory of God! Meanwhile your anointing is of great use for those who remain on earth. So don't let it go to waste like Elisha did, buried underneath the ground with your bones!

Much of what you carry spiritually can be passed along. Multiply the impact of the anointing you carry today by sending it down through the generations of families and of leaders. Pass that baton while you still can.

'mantle' of ministry from one person to another.

101   2 Timothy 1:6

CHAPTER 11

Timing is Everything

——

Sprinting with an arm outstretched and delivering a metal cylinder directly into the hand of another runner whose arm is trailing behind him as he runs ever faster down the track is a tricky endeavor.
Sports writer Kerrie Gillespie[102]

The right thing done at the wrong time often becomes the wrong thing. In baseball the difference between a homerun and a strikeout is sometimes just a matter of split-second timing. A batter must the judge the speed and type of each pitch in order to make correct contact with the ball. The right swing a little early or late becomes the *wrong swing.* The same thing applies to a relay race. Passing the baton between runners sounds easy, until you consider the following: The incoming runner is slowing down, while the outgoing runner is speeding up. One is operating by sight and sound, while the other is operating by feel. The incoming runner is extending the baton in one hand while the other reaches back with the opposite hand, hoping to feel the baton being pressed into it. All this must take place between narrow lane boundaries within a 20 metre exchange zone in about two seconds. To get it right takes practice, cooperation and *precise timing.* A little early or late and the entire team suffers a setback.

Don't Miss the Moment
When it comes to organizational leadership, whether that be sports, business, politics or ministry, leaders often miss the ideal moment for a transition. *Why?* One reason is our constant *sense of hurry.* From YouTube videos to Instagram, Twitter, Facebook and Snapchat, modern means of communication which increasingly chop up our time into smaller pieces. 'Time is running out', we think to ourselves, 'I need to double up on my 'To Do' List!'

---

102   Toronto Star – Sports Section August 11, 2017, accessed online at www.thestar.ca March 2018

That view of time produces chronic short-term thinking. It impairs our vision when making important decisions. Most of the bad decisions I have made in my life have to do with hurry or short-term thinking. I take some comfort in the fact that I'm not alone. Even genius strategists like billionaire Eric Schmidt, executive chairman of Alphabet, the parent company of Google, have admitted this weakness,

> "I find almost everybody, including myself, makes the mistake of making a short-term decision without thinking of a strategy for five years… For anything important, put it in a five-year context."[103]

People don't become billionaires because they are great multi-taskers. Those who build wealth through honest means are the type who think and see ahead so that they know what to do in advance. Those who make great transitions have planned well and are not in a hurry. Let me put it this way. Time is not running out. Time is *coming toward you*. Every day it delivers a fresh batch of hours and minutes to your doorstep free of charge. They are yours to use wisely for the good of yourself and others. There will always be enough time to do God's will God's way. Take a deep breath and declare the death of hurry in your life!

Those who make great transitions have planned well and are not in a hurry.

When it comes to families and faith, hurry is a thief that robs parents and children of those all-important teachable moments which make up the baton pass of faith. Transferring the faith is a process that spans many years, however much of the work occurs in short instalments. At certain moments in everyday life, events occur that briefly turn the mind and heart of a young person to eternal questions. Parents must recognize and capitalize on these brief windows of opportunity to speak into the lives of their children. The

---

103   from an interview with CNBC reported on cnbc.com April 11, 2017

baton pass of faith between generations is made up of hundreds of these teachable moments throughout early childhood and into adolescence.

At the other end of the scale is *complacency*. Although it is less common, it still needs to be mentioned. Some middle-aged to senior-aged leaders are doing 'just fine, thank you' and like things just the way they are. Some leaders have been so blessed or successful that their ministries are on cruise control and they are not planning for the inevitable transition. They think to themselves, '*I am not ready for the hassle of having to plan for something new at my age.*' If that's you, I hope this book is your alarm clock!

> The baton pass of faith between generations is made up of hundreds of teachable moments.

Another more common reason for missing the moment is what I will call *plodding without planning*. I heard Leadership Consultant John Maxwell tell the following anecdote at a Leaders' Conference. A pastor of a small church was complaining to John about a lack of growth and momentum in his church. "I don't know why it's like this," the pastor moaned, "after all, I have *ten years'* experience." John replied, "You don't have ten years' experience, you have *one* year's experience *ten times!*" Maxwell hit the nail on the head. Some leaders are really just plodders giving their full attention to whatever presents itself to them that week. They don't think ahead and therefore aren't prepared for the important moments of growth or transition.

Let me tell you a fishing story to make the point: it's about one that almost got away. Our eldest son, David loves sports and fishing. When he was attending university, we would often take road trips to Major League Baseball parks. On one of those trips, we stopped to fish in a large lake. As per usual, I was not catching much and when it started to rain, we quit early and dropped by unannounced on a nearby pastor friend of mine. Pastor Bob (as I will call him) had been serving his church for fourteen years. He already past the official retirement age, so I asked him what his transition plans were. He responded with an embarrassed grin. Bob had been a great pastor, but he didn't have a plan on how it all should finish, so he just kept plodding.

I felt that a young man I was mentoring, named Chris, would be an ideal fit for this church as long as he had a little preparation for the role. Pastor Bob invited me to work with his leadership team and within three months, the young man was serving as their first assistant Pastor. Two years later the congregation voted him in as the new Senior Pastor. It ended up being one of the smoothest pastoral exchange zone experiences I have witnessed. Here's what Chris had to say about it:

> "At the time, I was finishing Bible college and looking for a pastoral job. Terry introduced me to Pastor Bob. God knit our hearts together, and it was decided that I would join the church for this unique process.
>
> I worked with Pastor Bob as his Associate Pastor for a year while Lead Pastor responsibilities were gradually transitioned onto my plate. I started off preaching once in a while, then monthly, then twice a month, and three times a month by the end. I first attended board meetings, then I co-led them, then I led them on my own with Bob present to watch. Bob graciously moved aside little by little, giving me his support as he did.
>
> Through it all, Pastor Bob was a constant, encouraging presence for me. There was nothing in him that felt threatened or anxious about someone younger moving in. For congregation members who weren't too sure about this inexperienced kid, Pastor Bob won them over. Due to our gradual transition, when our year together drew to a close, it simply felt like the most natural thing in the world for him to step aside and for me to slide into the Lead Pastor role officially.
>
> The benefits of this process were numerous. Everyone had a long time to get used to the idea. Nothing was jarring or surprising for the people. Rather than voting in a relative stranger as we often do, they were voting in someone they knew very well and already trusted."

If I had not been such a poor fisherman, perhaps this wonderful transition may never have occurred.

When Discouragement is a Good Thing

Leaders can become so emotionally connected to the ups and downs of life that they fail to notice the signs that say 'You are entering an Exchange Zone'. In order to get such a leader's attention, God may temporarily remove His enabling grace from their ministry. The leader becomes frustrated and discouraged, until he or she realizes that it's *transfer time*.

> God was no longer willing
> to give him grace to
> accomplish a task when it
> was time to give it away.

We have already talked about how Elijah passed his anointing to others. Now I want to briefly draw attention to the process God use to get Elijah's attention when it was time to transfer the leadership baton. Elijah had just triumphed in one of the greatest power encounters of all time. Outnumbered 450 to ONE, he had stared down the prophets of Baal and 'prayed down' fire upon a water-drenched altar. For an encore, he then prayed down rain on a sun-scorched land. Yet, just a few hours later, Elijah was disillusioned. He was depressed over the fact that his miracles had not brought an end to the ungodly reign of Ahab and Jezebel. During that moment, Elijah lost his perspective. Depression will do that to you. It skews your thinking and invites you to flirt with lies about yourself and the world around you. His strength was sapped because God was no longer willing to give him grace to accomplish a task when it was time to give it away. Elijah's discouragement had a purpose. It set him up for a crucial conversation that would convince him it was transfer time!

I recall a similar moment in my ministry life. Looking back, I wouldn't have missed it for the world as it set me up for the greatest transition of my life. The Spring of 2001 provided some highlights to our ministry. We had just finished our second forty day fast as a church.[104] The results were amazing and

---

104   In case this sounds too heroic, I should mention that I chose to fast on only 20

included one woman being instantly healed of widespread cancer (verified by x-ray). In my journal I wrote *'I have never seen such spiritual momentum in our church in all my years here'*. It would prove to be short-lived. By the summer I was getting uneasy as I started to sense a loss of momentum. By the Spring of 2002, I was as restless as a cat in a cage. The church was still alive with God's presence, but it had stopped growing. Something was not right and I could not put my finger on it. The fog of confusion rolled in preventing me from receiving future vision for the church family. My ministry mentor told me I was showing signs of depression. It offended my pride but it also spurred me to begin asking the right question *'Lord, is now the time for a transition?'*

In the summer of that year, I was slated to be one of the main speakers at a week-long conference for Pastors and their spouses held at a beautiful lakeside summer camp in Alberta. Due to my emotional condition, I considered cancelling. I didn't feel qualified to refresh anyone that month. Thankfully, after receiving prayer, I felt just enough strength to follow through. As Melissa and I boarded the plane, I had big questions and small expectations.

One morning at the camp, the Lord woke me up early and had a conversation with me. The conversation took place entirely within my thoughts but they were so strong and clear, that I knew that it was my Father in Heaven speaking. He made it clear that I was to resign as Pastor from our church and have no further leadership position. I remember hearing *"Resign your salaried position and title completely. No part-time position, no leadership role."* That evening I took Melissa out for dinner to break the news of what I had heard. I expected her to be surprised. No such thing. During dessert, Melissa looked at me between bites of our double-chocolate brownie and said, *'I already heard the same thing from God'*. Several additional confirmations came our way within 48 hours. I am always impressed at how God does that. The resulting transition was planned well and occurred over the next five months.

I should add that previous to the summer camp experience, I had presented a transition scenario to the leadership team that would have taken three to five years. It all made logical sense in my mind. I was still in my forties, we

---

out of 40 days. During this time I had several visions, but most were of food.

had just paid off the church debt and had recently increased our staff. Surely I had a few good years remaining in my role! But until I heard God's voice on the matter, I did not recognize that *I was already entering the exchange zone and in danger of missing God's timing.*

The voice of God was not limited to my resignation. Heavenly Father also made it clear that the leadership team should bring two Pastors on staff to coincide with my departure. So after the congregation voted on the new Senior Pastor, we called on a young emerging leader to also join the team. His name is Matt Tapley and after serving in an associate role for several years, Matt became the next Senior Pastor. Under his leadership, Lakemount has grown in influence beyond all of our expectations. (At the time of writing, Matt is still my Pastor.)

I have often wondered how much more complicated the transition would have been if I had missed the message that my Heavenly Father was sending me during those turbulent few months? What if my momentary depression had been misread as a character flaw or the devil's victory? What kind of non-productive detour might my life have taken at that point? (Unfortunately I can probably answer that question from the examples of leaders I know who missed the signs, and the timing, of a needed transition.)

To run your race well, you must read the signs sent by God. A missed baton pass always sets your team back. If a transition is somewhere on the horizon for you, ask God to speak to you about the timing. Don't be in a hurry. But don't wait long enough to get depressed about it.

CHAPTER 12

Other-Centered Living

We cannot hold onto the batons of ministry
as though the baton is the trophy itself.
The trophy is won after this life.
Pastor Matt Tapley, Lakemount Worship Centre

Looking Out For Number Two

We expect self-centered behavior in certain environments. For example, when competing for a scholarship or playing the game of Scrabble, it's all about someone losing so the other can win. Many times our place of employment can feel like that too. When I worked for a computer manufacturer, I recall once that a false rumour was spread about me by someone trying to get a special travel assignment that had already been promised to me. It worked. I soon learned that in order to get ahead in that work environment, *'looking out for number one'* had to be the top priority.

In a relay race, that attitude never produces a winner. Success is accomplished by *helping the next one* that follows you. To bring this point home, I want to take you to a different kind of relay race. You will need to take off your spiked shoes for a few moments and put on a pair of skates. And you may want to put on an extra layer as well, as we go from the rubberized track to the ice rink…

> In a relay race, success is
> accomplished by helping the
> next one that follows you.

In the short-track speed skating relay, team members take turns doing multiple laps on a short oval, one at a time. The skater currently on the track is often 'covered' by the next skater. The next skater will actually match the current skater's progress by skating a smaller circular route inside the racing lanes while waiting for the optimum moment to jump into the race. The exchange zone is not marked on the ice, but can occur at *any time the two skaters agree* that the current one is ready to be replaced. When the sign is given, the next skater moves outward from the inner area to the skating lane where they must touch before the new skater can surge ahead. That 'touch' involves a helpful push. The new skater will briefly crouch in front of the outgoing skater to *receive a push from behind* in order to acquire maximum speed as fast as possible. The touch should take place while both skaters have synced their pace *and the outgoing skater still has enough energy* to give the incoming skater a strategic push. If the outgoing skater has used up all her energy on her own laps, staying in the lane until she is totally 'gassed', then she will not be able to set up the next skater for maximum performance. That little push can make a big difference to the outcome of the race. That little push says:

> 'I am ready to give you my lane'

> 'I am thinking about how to help you get into the race'

> 'I have reserved some energy to help give you a quick start!'

Too often in life, work and ministry, that 'little push' is noticeably absent. Children become adults without significant input or assistance from their parents. And many times, leaders assume positions of authority receiving little more than a pocketful of good wishes from the previous leaders. Too often the strategic push is absent and the opportunity for excellence is forfeited.

Calling All Spiritual Mothers and Fathers

What we need are people who understand how to live with the attitude of a mother and father. The Apostle Paul is the one who said 'You have many teachers but not many fathers.'[105] The Apostle John went further and identified three different levels of spiritual maturity - children, young men and fathers[106] (this could also read young women and mothers). This has little to do with someone's age. For example, a mature teenager can be acting as a spiritual mother or father for a younger person who is a new Christian. Meanwhile, I know many middle-aged men who are still operating with the maturity level of a 'young man'. Each stage has its charm and also its

---

105   1 Corinthians 4:15

106   1 John 2:13

characteristic behavior. Children are cute but always need to be led and fed. Young people are strong but often competitive and proud. Fathers and Meanwhile, mothers and fathers are all about their children. Their raison d'etre is the well-being of the next generation.

> ## Sometimes even spiritual mothers and fathers have trouble letting go of their cherished dreams.

Sometimes even spiritual mothers and fathers have trouble letting go of their cherished dreams. Moses begged God to allow him to cross over the Jordan River even though he had already groomed a younger man, Joshua, for that task. Moses had paid such a high price to get to the brink of the Promised Land, it only seemed fair that he should get to *keep* going. Moses must have spent quite some time bothering God about this as you can see from his candid inclusion of God's reply:

> *"'That is enough,' the Lord said.' Do not speak to me anymore about this matter.... Look at the land with your own eyes, since you are not going to cross this Jordan. But commission Joshua, and encourage and strengthen him, for he will lead this people across and will cause them to inherit the land that you will see'.*"[107]

That stern reminder rescued Moses from his self-centered attitude. He relented and commissioned Joshua to take over at the river crossing.

Biggest Bible Fails

Unlike Moses, some leaders don't listen to God and *do fail to set up the next generation for success.* Here are two of the biggest fails in fathering found in the Bible. The lessons contained in these stories are relevant, powerful and up to date. Both are family stories, with nationwide consequences. Both provide painful pictures of how good it might have been but how bad it actually became through mere negligence.

---

107   Deuteronomy 3:23 – 28

The first story is about Solomon and his son Rehoboam. David groomed Solomon for leadership and *listened to the voice of God to understand how and when to transfer his authority to him.* Perhaps you know that King David started out as the youngest and most neglected brother in a large family. It took an outsider, the prophet Samuel, to convince David's father Jesse, that David was qualified and ready to assume a leadership role. Perhaps David never forgot how it felt to be the one who was constantly overlooked and determined that he would pay attention to Solomon from the get-go. We will never know for sure. We do know that David set his son up for success. Solomon's renowned wisdom was a gift from God, but it was also the product of a father and mother who had it in their hearts to spend the time and energy to train him.[108] Over the course of his lifetime, Solomon's influence and wealth far exceeded that of his father. During Solomon's reign, Israel enjoyed more peace, larger boundaries and greater wealth than ever before.

Solomon only had one recorded son, Rehoboam. With no wars to fight, you'd think Solomon would have had ample time to do for his son what David had done for him. It does not seem to be the case. There are no records of interaction between Rehoboam and his father Solomon. Solomon had a massive amount of stuff including a fleet of ships, tens of thousands of animals and a yearly income of approximately one billion dollars. He also had a mind-boggling amount of women in his life; a *thousand* wives and concubines in total (*for the women reading - that would be the same amount of work as having ten husbands*). Solomon's possessions and relationships diverted his attention, consumed his time and reduced the flame of spiritual passion. Evidently these all became weapons of mass *distraction*.

What follows is one of the most disheartening moments in the history of King David's dynasty. When Rehoboam began his rule, he needed advice. Wouldn't you think he would take the counsel of his father's advisors, *who had worked with the wisest man in the known world?* No, Rehoboam rejected their advice and took the advice of "*the young men who had grown up with him.*"[109] That phrase, '*who had grown up with him*' is repeated twice and

---

108   Solomon testifies to this himself saying: "When I was a boy in my father's house, still tender and an only child of my mother, he taught me and said..." Proverbs 4:3-4

109   1 Kings 12:8-13

appears nowhere else in the Bible. It makes a powerful point. Rehoboam had spent more time with his friends than his father. Therefore he trusted his friends *more* than his father. Solomon was too busy to do for Rehoboam what David had done for Solomon. The consequences were monumental and generational. Lacking the requisite life experience and fatherly wisdom, Rehoboam treated the people so harshly that most rebelled against his leadership. The result was a virtual civil war. Israel was split in two and never reunited. If only Solomon had invested in his son the way his father and mother had invested in him, it is possible that the nation's history would have been forever changed.

The second story is one of the most jarring examples of self-centered leadership to be found in the Old Testament. King Hezekiah began to reign in Jerusalem when he was just 25 years old.[110] Unlike his father Ahaz, young Hezekiah served the Lord with all his heart.[111] He removed idol worship from the land. During a time of national crisis when Jerusalem was besieged by the Assyrians, Hezekiah learned how to seek God in earnest prayer. As a result, God miraculously delivered the city.

When Hezekiah was around forty years old, the prophet Isaiah predicted that he was soon to die. The Bible tells us that Hezekiah *"turned his face to the wall and prayed to the Lord... and wept bitterly."*[112] Hezekiah funneled his experience with God's faithfulness into a passionate prayer for his own life. God responded by adding 15 years to his lifespan. So far so good! But those additional 15 years produced some of Hezekiah's worst days as his heart grew proud. After showing off all the treasures in his storehouses to foreign visitors, Hezekiah was rebuked by God, through the prophet Isaiah. The words are chilling:

> *"The time will surely come when everything in your palace,*
> *and all that your fathers have stored up until this day, will*
> *be carried off to Babylon. Nothing will be left, says the Lord.*
> *And some of your descendants, your own flesh and blood, that*

---

110 2 Kings chapters 18 – 21

111 *"He did what was right in the eyes of the Lord, just as ... David had done."* 2 Kings 18:3

112 2 Kings 20:2 – 3

will be born to you, will be taken away And they will become eunuchs in the palace of the king of Babylon".[113]

What horrible news for a king or a father to be told! Obviously it was time for the great prayer warrior king to swing back into action. God had relented before, maybe earnest prayer could do it again. *That's not what happened.*

Does Hezekiah go to the temple of the Lord to earnestly plead for a different outcome?

Does he turn his face to the wall and weep bitterly?

Does he plead with God and ask for a sign?

None of the above.

In stark contrast to his response when he himself was about to die, Hezekiah seems almost relieved by Isaiah's words! " *'The word of the Lord you have spoken is good,' Hezekiah replied. For he thought 'will there not be peace and security in my lifetime?'"*[114]

Wow. It's hard to read those words coming from the mouth of a former hero. At this point in his life, Hezekiah seems concerned only for his own personal welfare. Though he had learned how to pray in faith during troubled times, there was no inclination in his heart to spend that faith on others, even his own descendents. Tragic!

Immediately we see the fortunes of Israel turning sour. Hezekiah's son Manasseh began to reign at the tender age of 12 years old. Manasseh was not born until three years after Hezekiah began his 15 year extension period. Manasseh would have no living memory of his father as an uncompromising king who purified the nation. His ears did not hear the earnest prayers of his father during the times of national crises. He did not hear the prophet and the people laud his father's fearless faith. What did Manasseh see when he

---

113   2 Kings 20: 16 – 18

114   2 Kings 20:19

looked at his father? A self-absorbed middle-aged man interested primarily in living out his last days in comfort.[115]

Hezekiah had somehow created a false finish line for the time he was to reign. It was as if he considered the additional fifteen years to be a 'bonus round' given to him to do as he pleased. Hezekiah was content to lay back and bask in the prosperity his earlier obedience had purchased. His energy was not reserved for the incoming leader. His thoughts were not turned toward the future generations. What a terrible price his family, and the nation, paid for Hezekiah's self-interest.

Who Are You Tracking With?

Returning to the short track skating relay, picture again what happens between the two skaters. The current one is pushing hard but aware that the next skater is 'tracking' her progress, imitating her stride on a shorter inside route. Her thoughts are on how to make the most of that moment when they will briefly skate together in the same lane. The next skater is on high alert, waiting with pent up energy for the signal to jump into the lane. These two are on the same team. They have talked about this moment and prepared together. Anticipation is high for a great transfer to take place.

> Find someone you can
> 'track' with who is already
> functioning in an area of life
> to which you are called.

For emerging generation leaders, I urge you to not just go your way because it feels like freedom. Try to find someone you can 'track' with who is already functioning in an area of life to which you are called. Talk to them about your dreams and desires. *If they take an interest in who you are becoming, then match their stride* and await your opportunity to enter the lane where you will receive that little push that gives you the competitive edge. That's what pregnant Mary did when no one understood who she was carrying. She ran to the hill country to stay with Aunt Elizabeth. Aunt Lizzie was

---

115   Hezekiah was around 55 years old when he died

happy to set aside the talk about her own pregnancy (John the Baptist) and call out the greater one within Mary (the Lord Jesus). *That little push gave Mary all the prophetic insight and encouragement she required to get into her destiny lane with full momentum.*

Just Say 'NO' to Bucket Lists

The final word here goes to people who have surpassed Hezekiah's maximum age (55 years old). What's up with all those 'bucket lists'? A bucket list refers to things you want to do before you die.[116] Usually it's really meaningful stuff like being the first to climb Mount Everest in a swimsuit. Sorry to say this, but living out of a bucket seems rather lame to me. Why would I need a bucket when I have a river!?[117] Seriously though, for all those planning or enjoying your retirement, how would your priorities shift if you knew that your greatest accomplishment in life may still be ahead of you? What would change on your bucket list if you knew there were world shapers eagerly waiting for you to put down your fishing rod and hand them a baton? Don't use up all your reserves planning your next cruise. Save some of it to launch a future leader. You might change the course of history.

---

116   Apparently the term 'kick the bucket' comes from an English old idiom for death by hanging. Convicts would stand on an overturned bucket and after the noose was applied someone would kick the bucket out from under their feet to leave them hanging in mid-air.

117   I'm talking about the river of God's presence and it is satisfying at every age and stage of life. Psalm 36:8 NIV 'you give them drink from your river of delights.'

CHAPTER 13

Next, Please

He must increase but I must decrease.
John the Baptist referring to the next leader, Jesus

A pastor friend of mine had reached official retirement age and was still the main leader in the church he had founded twenty-five years ago. One day I asked him, "So what are your transition plans? Who will be the next leader?" He seemed surprised by the question and then quickly replied, "I don't know, I haven't heard anything from God about it yet". Twenty-five years without giving thought to the next leader? If this was a game show, a loud buzzer would have sounded indicating WRONG ANSWER. But it's not a game. It's real life with real people needing someone to lead them in the midst of a rapidly changing world. When this man eventually retires, will he walk away and leave them to figure it out for themselves? There's no need for such a weak transition. I can guarantee you that *God already has the next leader in mind* and has been eager to share it with that man and his leadership team.

These Things are Spiritually Discerned

Some things cannot be figured out with our own brains. They must be revealed. We need the Holy Spirit. Recognizing future leaders that God has chosen is one of those things. Setting leaders in place absolutely requires the kind of discernment that is a direct gift from the Holy Spirit. We dare not rely solely upon our own wits.

Think back for just a moment to the Prophet Samuel choosing the next King. Even such a wise and seasoned man of God as Samuel got it wrong, seven out of eight attempts. When Samuel arrived at the home of Jesse, the family from whom the next anointed leader would be chosen, there were eight sons from which to pick. Samuel sized them all up and was ready to choose any one of the *other* sons of Jesse until God clearly spoke that David was the one to anoint. During that process God reminded Samuel, *"Man looks at the outward appearance, but the Lord looks at the heart."*[118]

Let's admit that we are not going to get it right most of the time when we use only a checklist to choose the next leader. The same thing goes for voting in the context of spiritual decisions. *You cannot vote someone into the will of God.* A life calling isn't decided by a committee. Too often churches, businesses and ministries rely primarily upon the world's means of selecting leaders. I am referring to the process of voting on an issue when there is an obvious lack of unified prayer and spiritual discernment involved in the process. It rarely works out well.

You cannot vote someone into the will of God.

Let's turn to Acts (chapter one) for an example of what I am talking about. Admittedly this is *my take* on the story. So please hear me out and you be the judge. The setting is the daily prayer gathering of the one hundred and twenty believers prayerfully waiting for God to do a 'new thing'.[119] Peter stands up in front of the group and announces that, with the sudden departure of Judas, there is a vacant leadership position to be filled. Quoting a prophecy from the Psalms, Peter indicates that God intends for another person to be added to the list of Apostles in Judas' place. So far so good. Then Peter moves from facts to presumption saying 'therefore it is necessary to choose one of the men who have been with us the whole time… One of these men must become a witness with us…'. *Was it necessary to choose someone right then, from that group?* The scripture had not spoken of the timing or the method, just the fact that Judas needed to be replaced. Peter is the one who added the sense of urgency. Peter and friends picked the familiar Old Testament method of 'casting lots' to choose. Drawing lots was a culturally accepted practice at that time. The soldiers at the foot of the Cross cast lots to decide who would receive Jesus' garment. And sometimes, under the Mosaic Law, lots would be cast to discern God's voice. *However, if Peter had waited just a few days, he would have been introduced to a whole new way of discerning*

---

118   1 Samuel 16:7

119   see Acts 1:15-26

God's will. Less than ten days later, Peter, newly filled with the Holy Spirit, would be flowing in words of knowledge and faith for physical healing. Instead, Peter and the leadership team fill the knowledge vacuum using the accepted 'business model' of casting lots. I think it is significant that the person they chose, Matthias, is never mentioned again.

It is my opinion that they should have just given it a rest, 'taken a chill pill', and waited upon the Holy Spirit to identify the *Next Generation* leader. I believe that person was most likely Paul the Apostle. God had pre-selected him and eventually *through a gift of the Spirit,* another person named Ananias would recognize who Paul was in God's eyes:

After Paul's supernatural encounter with Jesus on the road to Damascus, "... the Lord said to Ananias, 'Go! This man is my chosen instrument to carry my name before the Gentiles and their kings and before the people of Israel…"[120] Did you catch that? "My *chosen* instrument". God's choice for an additional Apostle was not determined by a roll of the dice. At the right time *God revealed it* through a gift of the Spirit.

Let's get this straight once and for all. Identifying the right person at the right time with the right calling, requires the Holy Spirit's direction. Voting may be used to *affirm* spiritual discernment but must never *replace* spiritual discernment. I have participated in many church-related votes, for board members, for pastors and for paving parking lots. We sure could have used less talk and more Holy Spirit on some of those occasions!

Spiritual Truths in Spiritual Words

The Bible clearly states that Spiritual truths formed into Spiritual words don't necessarily make sense to those without the Spirit of God in them.[121] Here's an up-to-date example from a close friend of mine, Dr. Grant Mullen, a former family physician. He and his wife Kathy played integral roles in the Holy Spirit renewal that occurred in our church. During that time, the Lord called Grant to give up his medical clinic and enter full time Christian ministry. Since then Grant and Kathy have written several books and traveled the world conducting seminars that bring people into physical, emotional

---

120   Acts 9:15 NIV

121   1 Corinthians 2:13-14

and spiritual health. Physical healings occur from time to time when they pray for people.

No one who knew Grant as a young man would have picked him for this kind of ministry. By his own confession Grant was given to cynicism and not the type you would expect to stand in front of people releasing faith for physical and emotional healing. Yet one person did discern the anointing hidden deep within Grant during that period of his life: the famous healing evangelist, Kathryn Kuhlman[122].

In 1968, teenaged Grant traveled to Pittsburgh to attend one of her weekly services at the Carnegie Music Hall. Grant and a few others were selected to join the on stage to receive prayer. Ms. Kuhlman prayed one of her standard prayers for each one until she laid her hand on upon Grant. At that moment, she exclaimed '*Oh … this young man has the Holy Spirit within him!*' This would have sounded like a generic statement if spoken by most other people. However coming from the lips of a woman so gifted by God and *so tuned in to the Holy Spirit's miracle working agenda*, these words had significance. I believe that Ms. Kuhlman was carrying such a strong anointing for healing that *her spirit was able to recognize a similar anointing upon others*. Her words represented a recognition *by the Holy Spirit* that Grant was already carrying a Spiritual anointing (resident authority and ability) in the area of healing. This anointing was not yet visible to the natural eye but it was there.

Over the next two decades, you would have been hard pressed to see the clues of this call upon Grant. There were no signs of miracle working power in his life. However '*God's gift and his call are irrevocable*'[123] and twenty years later, Grant and Kathy began to see the evidence of what the Spirit had witnessed to decades earlier. What struck me most when Grant told me about all of this was *the lingering impact of that brief spiritual endorsement* and how it seemed to compensate for other life experiences where people who should have recognized the call on his life, failed to do so.

---

122   Whatever your take on healing evangelists, please keep in mind that Kathryn Kuhlman's ministry produced more documented cases of inexplicable improvements in serious medical conditions than anyone else in the twentieth century. Her delivery was often theatrical but the results were phenomenal.

123   Romans 11:29 NIV

If we are going to raise up a generation of world shapers, we better get our spiritual discernment tuned up. We must become familiar with that still small voice, that witness of the Spirit, that Holy 'YES' in our heart that God so often gives discerning people when they encounter anointed leaders-in-waiting. Education and life experience are important, but they do not always give us the ability to see what God knows about a person's future potential. Being able to recognize someone *according to the Spirit* and call forth their future destiny is essential for setting up the next generation to do the 'greater works' that Jesus talked about.

As the saying goes, 'the cream always rises to the top'. A person who is anointed by God cannot be kept on the sidelines forever. He or she will rise to their calling eventually, regardless of how they may be viewed by those who lack spiritual discernment. No one could stop the Apostle Paul's inevitable rise. However, it took many years for Paul to be accepted as an Apostle by the other eleven. I wonder how that might have changed if the eleven Apostles had waited to be filled with the Holy Spirit before making the decision to replace Judas.

> A person who is anointed
> by God cannot be kept on
> the sidelines forever.

Personally, I also feel that in the absence of Spirit-filled parents, and lacking a mentor for many years, the pathway to my destiny was longer and more arduous than it might have been otherwise. Thank God for Pastor George Tunks who did recognize me according to the Spirit as a twenty-one year old immature follower of Christ. I want to do the same for the emerging generations.

The Next One May be the Next *Ten*

I believe that these are days of multiplication. We do not need to add leaders, we need to *multiply* the number of leaders. The Great Commission is probably a lot greater than we thought. Jesus didn't just intend for us to make disciples *in* all nations, He actually told us to make disciples *of* all nations. (Matthew 28:18) That one word changes a lot. Is it possible to disciple a nation? What does that mean? It's hard to get our minds around that concept so we tend to reduce it to 'in all nations.' Ah yes, I can handle that - go and make a few disciples in every nation. That makes sense. But that's not the end game. Jesus was looking beyond our day to the day when *the nations will pay Him tribute.*[124] As the day of His return draws closer, I believe that we will see major cultural shifts as whole communities and even certain groups turn away from ungodly beliefs to embrace the Gospel and a Bible-based lifestyle. In my lifetime more people have come to saving faith in the Lord Jesus Christ than in all the prior centuries combined. That's due to two factors: the rate of growth of the world population and the rate of growth of Spirit-filled Christianity. Today, Christianity is growing rapidly in many parts of the world.[125] Yet I believe that 'we ain't seen nothin' yet'! The number of prayer movements today is beyond control in a good way! We are witnessing days of fruitful increase, preparing us for the Lord's return. Leaders who are in step with the Holy Spirit's agenda will be preparing to pass their baton of anointing and authority not just to one person, but to many. Like Elijah who anointed three in his place, the culture around us will begin to shift when we multiply our impact by passing the baton to many, not just one.

People who have been on the front lines of world evangelism know this to be true. Even way back in 1974, Billy Graham sensed that the times were changing and that the evangelical message would be carried forward not by just one religious superstar but by armies of preachers around the world. It was reported that when "he was attending the International Congress on World Evangelization in Lausanne, Switzerland. Someone asked him the question: Who will be the next Billy Graham? He answered by pointing to the gathering before him of 2,300 Christian leaders from 150 countries. "They will," he said."[126]Graham didn't expect all 2,300 attendees to have the

---

124   In Psalm 2:8, God the Father is prophetically speaking to Jesus. Revelation 7:9-10 is part of the fulfilment of what the Father promised.

125   For example, the documented number of Pentecostal-Charismatic Christians has risen from a merely a scattered few to well over 500 million in the past 120 years. In China even the government itself estimates that over a hundred million persons have converted Christianity in the past seventy years. Tens of millions more have been 'born again' in Argentina, Indonesia and Africa in the same timeframe.

126   From the Charlotte Observer online accessed May 2018
http://www.charlotteobserver.com/living/religion/article148653099.html#storylink=cpy

same gift and calling as his own, but he was making an essential point... The next ONE may be the next TEN.

> If you are quietly waiting
> in the wings for your turn,
> then consider following the
> example of Joshua.

Just Do It!

It's time. We are overdue to recognize and release the true Spiritual anointing upon the incoming generation. If you are quietly waiting in the wings for your turn, then consider following the example of Joshua. He stayed longer than any of his peers at the places where God's Spirit was strongly present. He constantly hung out with the anointed leader of his day. Do the same because your turn is coming.

If you are due to pass the baton, don't get caught up in methodology. There is no one divinely sanctioned method for appointing leaders or choosing people for godly tasks. Any method can be used by God (even voting) as long as *spiritual discernment* and the *voice of the Holy Spirit* are part of the equation. Whatever you are doing in life, you have the right and the responsibility to ask God to show you who's next in line to carry your Spiritual authority. Expect the Lord to reveal it to you. Pray for it, discern it, and plan for it. And then just go and do it!

PART FOUR
An Unstoppable Life
––––––

It is possible to live in such a way that the Blessings resting upon one life are transferred to the lives of others for many generations. Part Four reveals three key components for making this a reality in your life.

Chapter 14 When God Makes a Promise

This chapter reveals a deep and powerful truth. It has to do with your relationship with God's promise to Father Abraham. In this chapter all political viewpoints of modern day Israel are temporarily set aside in order to think of Israel only as *Abraham's family*.

Chapter 15 Telling Your Story

This chapter reveals and examines time-tested methods for creating spiritual momentum within your family.

Chapter 16 Unstoppable Prayers

This chapter lays down two foundational principles for effective praying:

How to get answers that span generations and how to go beyond what you normally would ask or think.

Chapter 17 The Anchor Leg

This chapter sums up our great relay race of faith with a brief inspirational message based upon Hebrews Chapter 12. Special attention is given to the final or 'Anchor Leg' of your race.

CHAPTER 14

When God Makes a Promise

———

I've written twelve novels and I've found out that
fiction can't keep up with real life.
John Grisham

Welcome to one of the most unusual stories of my life.

Long before I understood the concepts shared in this book, the Lord graciously revealed the power of passing a blessing between generations. I now understand that blessing Israel will powerfully connect us with the Thousand Generation Covenant of God's we talked about in Chapter Three. Therefore it is an essential component of our relay race of faith.

What you will read in this chapter is best described as a Holy Spirit 'intervention' into my belief system. It changed my relationship to Abraham and his offspring and connected me to the most influential promise ever made :

> *The Lord had said to Abram,*
> *"Go from your country, your people*
> *and your father's household*
> *to the land I will show you.*
> *"I will make you into a great nation,*
> *and I will bless you;*
> *I will make your name great,*
> *and you will be a blessing.*
> *I will bless those who bless you,*
> *and whoever curses you I will curse;*
> *and all peoples on earth*
> *will be blessed through you."*
> Genesis 12:1-3

"You must go to Israel!"

Those words, spoken to me by a well-meaning friend, did not land well on my heart. It wasn't the first time that someone had tried to get me to go to Israel, so I was armed and ready with my pushback response -

> *"Thanks for the advice, but I just don't have a burden for Israel. You have a burden for that nation and I have a burden for other nations like China. The Lord said to go and make disciples of all nations, and so we all have a different focus."*

Although I felt quite satisfied with my logic, I could tell that my friend was not at all moved from his conviction. Why couldn't people like him just accept the fact that I was not interested? I had no anti-Semitic feelings, but the land of Israel carried no particular fascination for me, especially as it related to the fulfillment of Old Testament prophecy. I felt that it too was easy for people like my friend to mix up the Old and the New Covenants. As far as I was concerned, Old Covenant promises were out of date due to the fact that Christians are living under the New Covenant, the *better* covenant according to Hebrews 7:22. I imagined my feelings were similar to the Apostle Paul when he responded to the legalistic Christians of his day with a sigh of frustration saying, "*understand then*, that those who have faith are children of Abraham".[127]

The most frustrating part of this Israel thing to me was dealing with the ultra-prophetic type people. You know, the ones who are always interpreting the latest newscast in light of end-times prophecy. Invariably they have an inordinate fascination with every newsy tidbit connected with the Middle East. I was not about to spend time and money crossing the ocean merely to placate the prophetic crowd.

Then, *it* happened. And just like that, I became ensnared in a threefold cord of coincidence, conviction and my wife's laser beam intuition...

The Junk Mail that Changed my Ministry

In November 1998, someone placed a piece of junk mail on my office desk. It advertised a familiarization tour for pastors and leaders to Israel. ('Fam Tours'

---

127   Galatians 3:7 emphasis mine

as they are called, are cut rate group trips subsidized by the government of Israel and tour companies in order to entice Pastors to sponsor their own group tours.) My secretary had opened the mail and left it there for me to read. The piece about the Israel trip caught my eye. Once I read it, I had a nagging feeling somewhere down deep that I should consider going. Maybe it was because the price was astonishingly cheap. But that little pushback voice in my mind immediately began to argue against the idea. "Ah yes, *that's the plan*, get me over there and put on the hard sell to lead my own tour." Upon reading the fine print, I was disappointed to discover that there were actually no strings attached to this offer.

The next step proved fatal to my resistance – I told my wife Melissa about it. Immediately her "spiritual radar" sounded in that special place within her soul where she and Jesus hang out. By the following day she was saying things like, "I think you should consider going. This might be the right thing at this time". By that point in our marriage I should've learned that those words *actually meant* " I *know* in my spirit that God wants you to go and I am not changing my mind. Meanwhile I will kindly but persistently wait for you to catch up to my insight."

Now that it was evident that my wife felt it was God's will for me to go to Israel, I decided to look for support in defense of my position in the Scriptures. 2 Corinthians 13:1 would do nicely: "every matter must be established by the testimony of two or three witnesses". In my heart, I did *not want to receive any confirmation* so I let the issue drop. And I purposely let the deadline pass for putting down the deposit on the trip. Finally at the urging of the Holy Spirit (and my wife), I called the tour company. I was expecting to hear "sorry about that, if only you had called two weeks ago…". Instead the tour leader, who happened to answer the phone, said to me, "well wouldn't you know, we have booked a 747 and there is just one seat remaining! *You called just in time*." Unfortunately I had received my "second witness". Here we were, a month after the deadline, and there was still one seat remaining on a 400 seat aircraft! I gave in and prayed, "*Yes Lord, I will go where you tell me to go*". My wife is a mature individual. When I shared what had happened, Melissa never said "I told you so". But there was a conspicuous smile on her face for a couple of days following.

In the weeks leading up to my trip, I began to have some unusual thoughts and impressions. I had long since learned that this was often the way God speaks to me but it was taking me time to process what I was hearing in my mind. First, I felt that the Lord was telling me that I was to go on this trip *in order to bless Israel*. Today that would make total sense to me, but at that time it confused me. I really had no idea what that would look like. From the pulpit one Sunday morning I requested congregational prayer to help me discern what I was supposed to do. In my awkwardness, I recall making a lame joke about mimicking Moses at Mount Nebo raising my hands and pronouncing a blessing while looking across the Jordan.

The other impression I had was to take the book *Oliver Twist* to read on the plane. Written by the famous 19th century British author Charles Dickens, the book centers on the story of an orphaned boy. Born in a workhouse, Oliver ends up on the streets of London in the grip of a gang of juvenile pickpockets led by the elderly criminal, Fagin. It was definitely a weird choice, but I couldn't shake the impression. With the systems analyst within me rolling his eyes, I decided to take this old fashioned florid novel in my carry on luggage to see what I might learn from a 'quick speed read'.

As the flight from Toronto to Tel Aviv reached cruising altitude, I covertly reached for Dickens' book thinking, "I must be the only pastor who has ever brought Oliver Twist with him on a trip to The Holy Land." I actually was not unfamiliar with the book or the author. I am of British descent and my mother's family had revered Charles Dickens. My mother, an avid reader, often told me that he was one of the greatest authors in the world. A golden bound set of Dickens complete works was prominently displayed on the living room mantel in my childhood home for as long as I could remember. The books never interested me. They contained too many adjectives and not enough action for a young boy. Now as I finally began to read Oliver Twist for myself, I was struck by the constant reference to the villain of the story, Fagin, as "*the Jew*" in an apparently derogatory manner. When Fagin is introduced for the first time, he is described as "*a very old and shrivelled Jew, whose villainous-looking and repulsive face was obscured by a quantity of matted red hair. He was dressed in a greasy flannel gown with his throat bare.*"[128] In this passage, Dickens refers to Fagin as 'the Jew' seven times and continues to

---

128   http://www.literaturepage.com/read/olivertwist-64.html accessed April 2018

prefer that term rather than his name for much of the book. Dickens was a true "wordsmith" who painstakingly painted vivid word pictures to support his narrative. There was no doubt in my mind that the repetitive use of the phrase "the Jew" was intentional in order to emphasize the nastiness of this villain. I set the book down and had a discussion with my own thoughts;

> *"There is a message here… Charles Dickens was anti-*
> *Semitic.*
> *It's funny I should discover that en route to Israel.*
> *But perhaps he wasn't even a Christian.*
> *Regardless, what possible significance could this man's*
> *anti-Semitism have for my life today?"*

In a few short days I would have an astoundingly direct answer to that question.

Meanwhile, I was still battling a case of mild disdain for people who were too enthusiastic about the land of Israel. In hindsight I realize that God had a double agenda on this trip. In addition to revealing my relationship to Abraham's promise, He was also exposing some impurities in my heart. One of the tools He used to begin this heart surgery was the Suitcase Lady. Let me introduce her to you…

After stepping off the plane in Tel Aviv, our tour group gathered at the luggage carousel. One member of this eclectic group was a woman dressed as if she was on her way to a friend's wedding. She eagerly welcomed two humongous suitcases, one of which I suspected was actually a small house trailer with the hitch removed. As we waited for the bus, she and I engaged in small talk which went something like this:

> ME: (calmly) *Is this your first trip to Israel?*

> Suitcase Lady: (with much enthusiasm) *Oh no I have been here 4 times already!*

> ME: (trying to sound interested) *How about that! And what keeps drawing you back?*

> Suitcase Lady: (bewildered at my ignorance) *'Why this is our home!"*

> ME: (inserting fake emotion and trying to not roll my eyes) '*Of course it is.*'

Having made a mental note to avoid further small talk with the Suitcase Lady and any other 'extremist' in the tour, I looked for someone I could team up with for the rest of the trip. I found a Baptist Pastor with whom I hit it off and felt safe again. He didn't seem the least bit fanatical.

This was going to be a whirlwind trip, designed to give the broadest experience in the shortest time possible. We stayed in six different locations in seven days and each day was crammed full of bus rides and tourist stops. I was eager to see many of the 'authentic' sites, (including *both places* where Jesus died.[129]) Meanwhile I needed to find a way to 'bless' Israel to make good on my statement back home. I had no clue how that would happen.

For a few days the routine was similar - wake up early, pack your suitcase (or travel trailer) before breakfast. Eat a great Mediterranean breakfast, board the bus, and try to hear the tour-guide's garbled voice on the microphone describing the next historical site. Then - get off the bus, listen to some interesting Biblical information and take pictures until the order came '*Back on the bus!*' In the evening, eat a great Mediterranean supper and talk about the most meaningful event of the day - which on one day was a debate on whether the army tank crossing in front of us was a Sherman or Abrams model. Our total free time on the tour was four hours one afternoon. At this point I had been fasting for two days to discern the voice of the Lord. It had been impressive to visit the remarkably intact historical sights, and see the remnants of early Christianity. I had even made a decision about which site was the authentic crucifixion site. As I walked alone though the streets of old Jerusalem, there was a growing feeling that perhaps the Israel enthusiasts around me might be onto something. What might the Suitcase Lady know that I didn't (other than why six pairs of high heels are mandatory on a tour of Israel)?

Alone with my thoughts, I noticed a sign on one of the shops which read "Used English Books". No more than 12 feet wide, its walls were lined with

---

129   As with many of the historical sites in Israel there is some level of doubt as to the precise location of Jesus' crucifixion. Two main sites are popular today.

Stephen King novels and the like. But there directly in front of me on the only table in the shop, was a book by Charles Dickens entitled *The Life of Our Lord*. There it was! Surely this was the missing clue required to solve my mystery. The price was three US dollars, which matched the money remaining in my pocket. So, of course I bought the book... *except I didn't*. Not buying that book, must rank as one of my all time greatest 'brain cramps'. You see, I had planned to end my food fast at 5 PM. I had made a mental note to save the three dollars in my pocket to purchase a shish-kebab I had spied being grilled just down the road. And so ironically, *while gazing at the possible answer to my prayer,* I had a vision...of eating shish-kebab. I rationalized to myself that I could go eat the kebab, find an ATM, take out more money, come back and buy the book, and scamper back to my hotel within the time permitted. Great plan! Alas, I could not find an ATM anywhere and had to return to my hotel without purchasing the book. (I now have a lot more sympathy for Esau who sold his birthright for some stew.)

The next morning at breakfast I shared my frustration with those at my table. I was trying to laugh off my embarrassment when a British Pastor seated at the table said, "I know that book". He continued, "I can assure you that Charles Dickens was a Christian. However he was also anti-Semitic. It seems that he may have subscribed to the British Israelite heresy."[130] So it wasn't the book itself I needed to examine.[131] God just had it placed there as a conversation starter leading me to this man who was well acquainted with Dickens' life story. The message from Heavenly Father to Terry Bone had to do with the fact that though many people are drawn to the life and teachings of Jesus, some still permit themselves to hold negative views of Jewish people in general (anti-Semitism). Immediately my heart witnessed

---

130   'British Israelite' refers to a form of 'Replacement Theology', the belief that the Jews forfeited their chance to welcome the Messiah (Jesus) when He came to earth the first time. Therefore they have all the curses and those who believe in Jesus get all their intended blessings. British Israelites actually believe that the Ten Lost Tribes of Israel are largely represented in Britain's population today. Herbert W. Armstrong popularized this belief through his Worldwide Church of God movement in the 1960s.
       You can read a summary of this at https://en.wikipedia.org/wiki/British_Israelism

131   I did get a copy of this book and read through it. Nothing Dickens says in the story is overtly anti-Semitic. This info comes from other sources. It is the fact that he could write so beautifully about Jesus in this book while at the same time holding a disparaging view of the Jews that became the relevant insight.

to the fact that my family was guilty of this. I would describe both my parents as *lightly* anti-Semitic. Mostly they just parroted the prevailing cultural sentiments of their day. To our family, a disparaging comment here or there about Jews in general didn't even qualify as a minor offence. But now I saw that it was anything but. And my mother had revered Dickens, embracing his writings uncritically.

I was reminded what God had said to Abraham: "*I will bless those who bless you*".

We bless or curse Abraham by the way we treat his descendants.

In the book of Romans, Paul, the former Pharisee and expert in Jewish law addresses this issue. He leaves no doubt that Abraham is the *father* of all those who are justified by faith. God's promise to Abraham *preceded* and *superseded* the Old Testament law. Therefore we still need to 'bless Abraham' today.[132] Until we do so, we have not yet aligned ourselves with God's unchangeable, unstoppable purpose for every family on earth. In another passage Paul asserts that the work of Jesus includes a grafting into that same promise:

> '*He redeemed us in order that the blessing given to Abraham might come to the Gentiles through Christ Jesus.*'[133]

Now I understood that merely 'not cursing' Abraham's children was not good enough. Something was out of alignment in my ancestry and in my indifference towards Abraham's descendants. We bless or curse Abraham *by the way we treat his descendants*. The fence that divides blessing and cursing had now become very uncomfortable for me to straddle. I needed to hop down and join the blessing side by doing two things:

> First, ask forgiveness on behalf of my family for failing to bless Abraham.

---

132   See Romans chapters 4 and 5

133   Galatians 3:14

Second, find some of Abe's descendants to bless!

I did the first immediately. It took less than two minutes and I felt no accompanying emotions as I prayed. (I have learned that feelings don't always immediately accompany obedience, but eventually they do come).

Two days later, our tour climbed Masada, the ancient fortress on a plateau 400 metres above the Dead Sea shore. This is the location where more than 900 Jews committed suicide just before the Roman Army's siege ramps finally breached the fortress wall, the final barrier in their mission to eradicate the Jewish population living there. This occurred around 73 A.D. shortly after the fall of Jerusalem.[134] At one point I let the tour move on and stood in the remnant of the 2,000 year old Jewish synagogue on that plateau. A portion of the Dead Sea Scrolls predicting the resurrection of the nation of Israel had been discovered at that exact spot a few decades earlier. I was taking in the significance of it all when an Orthodox Jewish family of four came and stood next to me. I turned to them and said,

> *"Excuse me, can I speak with you for a moment? I need to apologize - actually, repent - for what my people have done to your people. I am British and my people and my family have dishonored you and the covenant to your Father Abraham. I am truly sorry. This was wrong."*
>
> *The father tried to brush it off at first saying, "Don't worry. That was a long time ago."*
>
> *I insisted. "No, it's important. Will you please forgive us?"*
>
> *They paused for a moment then said, "Yes, we do."*
>
> *I continued: "I bless you, your family and your people. Thank you for recording and preserving the scriptures for people like me. We owe you a debt. Thank you."*

---

134   The story is exquisitely detailed by Josephus the historian. It's a fascinating story, more than worth the time to read and easily found by Googling the words Masada and Josephus.

*With those words, the mother and father seemed to understand
the depth of what I was trying to express. They each reached
out one hand and said, 'We bless you as well!'"*

That was all. They moved on, and I went to find the tour guide to tell him
what happened. Two sentences into the story I broke down sobbing convul-
sively. It flowed from deep within my spirit. I was FEELING God's sorrow
for His people. A flash of Old Testament Scriptures flooded my mind. *Now
I knew what those prophets were talking about!*

It was almost like a conversion experience. The rest of my trip was transformed
into a deeply emotional and spiritual journey. As I visited more sites, I dug
into the history and meaning of each one. I even had a great conversation
with the Suitcase Lady.

God's Order for Blessing Families

Back home I began to tell the story of blessing the people in Israel and how
it opened my eyes. And... yes... I also began to put plans in place to lead
my own tour. Three weeks later, I was asked to attend a weekend seminar
about Family Blessing based upon Jewish culture and the Bible. I decided
to attend and once I did, I saw the connection of the timing of the seminar
with my trip to Israel. After that weekend, I knew that Family Blessing would
become a life message for me and Melissa. It certainly has. Two decades later,
we have tens of thousands of books in print in five languages on the topic,
have taught it on national TV, and conducted seminars in many countries.
It has changed the course of our family life *for good.*

> One of the ways we
> create permanence in the
> generational transfer of
> faith is by blessing Abraham
> and his offspring.

I believe that my blessing Abraham's family was a prerequisite for God to
release to me the revelation of how family blessing works today. How could
He commission me to bring the revelation of Family Blessing to God's people

until I blessed God's premier family of faith? I had been a Christian for more than a quarter of a century before I realized that Genesis 12:1-3 was relevant to me. You might want to stop for a moment and ponder that thought.

I now believe that one of the ways we create permanence in the generational transfer of faith is by blessing Abraham and his offspring. I thank God for His mercy and determination which were both required to cause me to discover this essential truth. (There's a lot more to say about Genesis 12:1-3 with respect to *nations* being blessed. But that's another story for another book.)

Remember one of my first mentors I mentioned in Chapter One, Pastor George Tunks? He always said: "*You cannot be a Christian and have anything else in your heart except love for the Jews.*" I never understood why he said that so often from the pulpit. *Now I do.* Blessing Abraham's children is not the same as approving everything the modern political nation of Israel does. We can disagree with aggression and still bless Abraham. One of the ways we bless them best is to pray for the peace of Jerusalem as we are instructed in Psalm 122:6.

Let's do that together right now:
"Lord thank you for your unbroken promise to bless those that bless Abraham. As the father of all those who are justified by faith, we bless Abraham, his legacy and his descendants. We pray for the peace of Jerusalem and that You would bring Your people back to You and that they would see and understand that Jesus really is their Messiah." Amen.

CHAPTER 15

Telling Your Story

———

The testimonies of God are what connect
each succeeding generation of believers to His covenant.
Bill Johnson, Bethel Church, Redding CA

Along time ago, a Psalmist wrote these words,

"I will make your faithfulness known through all generations."

Is that really possible? Yes. It is. In this chapter, you will meet the man who wrote those words and discover the simple things you can do to send *your* story of God's faithfulness reverberating through the generations that follow.

Talk, Walk and Tie a Symbol

When the children of Israel were finally ready to cross the Jordan River into the promised land, they received a simple plan for intergenerational success. Moses was actually addressing the *second generation,* the children of those who had firsthand experience in being miraculously delivered. This generation had witnessed the great things that happened to their parents, but the whole 'God story' was in danger of extinction within one generation unless they followed the simple plan outlined to them. The specific steps to 'impress them upon your children' are summarized in Deuteronomy chapter 6:7-9,

- *Talk* about them when you sit at home

- And when you *walk* along the road, when you lie down and when you get up…

- Tie them as *symbols* on your hands and bind them on your foreheads…

- *Write* them on the doorframes of your houses and on your gates."

Telling your story is accomplished in four ways:

Talking it, Walking it, Picturing it and Recording it.

It comes as no surprise to me that these four elements closely match four learning styles identified by modern educators (for example VARK[135]) which are auditory, visual, reading/writing and kinesthetic (action and touch).

Talking is the preferred method for *auditory* learners, Walking for *kinesthetic* learners, Tying Symbols (Picturing) for *visual* learners and Writing is the obvious choice for *reading/writing* style learners.[136] When you go beyond your personal preference and include them all into your daily life, then, as the Bible tells us, it will have the effect of 'impressing' good and godly beliefs upon the souls of the next generation. Let's look at them one by one.

Talking Your Story

There is power in storytelling. For centuries, it has been the prime means of learning. Even today, with the advent of sophisticated media, life-like computer-generated images and the like, the highest grossing movies are still the ones with the best storylines. Nothing holds a person's attention like a great story. Jesus was a great teacher and for the most part, Jesus taught by telling stories. They were simply constructed tales using plain words that were easy to follow. Nothing complicated. Yet, *we are still re-telling those stories two thousand years later!* More than that, we are still learning from them.

Why do stories have such power to teach us? It is rooted in the truth that all learning comes from experience. Storytelling draws the listener into events as they unfold so that they vicariously experience what the people within

---

135   "Scientists and psychologists have developed a number of different models to understand the different ways that people learn best. One popular theory, the VARK model, identifies four primary types of learners: **visual, auditory, reading/writing, and kinesthetic.** Each learning type responds best to a different method of teaching." from https://blog.prezi.com/the-four-different-types-of-learners-and-what-they-mean-to-your-presentations-infographic/ April 2016

136   Everyone uses all four ways at some time or other, it's just that most of us prefer one style above the others.

the story experienced. In this manner the learning is passed on from teller to listener.

Everyone has a story to tell. God is at work in your life. God has blessed you and you *need* to tell others, especially those impressionable little ones growing up around you, if you are a parent. An additional benefit occurs as you speak to others about your story. Not only does your testimony bring them into a shared experienced, it also deepens your experience. As you repeat the story multiple times, you are actually creating neural pathways in your brain that imprint the story deeper into your mind.

> The 'God story' in your
> life story carries unlimited
> potential to bless others.

Some people tell me, '*Oh, but you don't have my story. I had such a painful past!*" Sorry, that excuse does not hold water. Centuries ago, a man named Jabez also had a painful past. The Bible tells us that his mother named him Jabez, which sounds like the word 'pain' in Hebrew, because she bore him in pain. What kind of pain? Physical or emotional? What about her husband? Was she a single parent? We do not know the answer to any of these questions. We do know however that Jabez was considered 'more honorable' than his brothers because he *refused to be defined by the pain of his past.* He called out to God for blessing, for increased influence and the ability to live in such a way that he would not cause others to have pain.[137] Jabez' story is found in an unlikely location - the midst of a census. In the middle of a prolonged and monotonous list of 'who gave birth to who', out pops the briefest of stories (comprised of a mere five sentences). The story is brief but the message is powerful and enduring. Many *centuries* later, the short prayer of Jabez became the subject of one of the fastest selling books in history![138]

---

137   1 Chronicles 4:9-10 are all we have to describe the life of Jabez. The NASB version concludes the brief vignette with the phrase '*that I might not cause pain*' which I believe is a better rendition than to be free of pain. It gives a clearer picture of the intent of the words.

138   *The Prayer of Jabez* book sold two million copies within the first two years after it was published. At the time of writing this book, the total copies of *The Prayer of Jabez* sold had surpassed ten million making it the fifth best selling Christian book of all time.

Here's my point: Your *pain* is *part* of your 'God story'. Don't deny it, run from it or hide it away. God wants to take the pain of your past and turn it into a powerful testimony. Once he has done that, the 'God story' in your life story carries *unlimited* potential to bless others. [139]

You also need to be telling those you love about *their God story*. We call this practice Family Blessing. All words are powerful but some are more powerful than others. The words of a sitting judge have legal authority. He or she has the power to change someone's life when speaking on behalf of the governmental authorities. Likewise, words of blessing actually release Heaven's authoritative power into people's lives.

Melissa and I wrote an entire book on this subject, entitled <u>The Family Blessing Guidebook</u>. It guides families through a process that brings the blessing and favor of God to our families and others with whom we have close relationship. One of the main ideas in that book is that *the Blessing and Favor of God is communicated from Heaven to earth through intentional words in the form of a blessing*. In fact, the very first family story in history began with a spoken blessing. Genesis 1:28 records that God's first words to Adam and Eve were as follows: "*He blessed them and said to them rule ...*"[140] Words have the ability to write a message on the hearts of people who love us. Parents, husbands, wives and singles, make sure you are writing the story of God's love and faithfulness on the hearts of those who are open to your words.

Walking Your Story

Deuteronomy says you need to be talking about your story 'when you *walk* along the road, when you lie down and when you get up...' As the saying goes, you need to 'walk the talk'. In other words, *don't segregate your teaching from your living*. Don't send your kids to Sunday School while you play golf. Don't just have a family devotional time, also talk and teach by example while you go through your normal routine. 'Do Life' together with the next generation!

When our eldest son David left home to attend university, it was a new experience for all of us. How would his faith withstand the constant barrage

---

139   More detail on this topic can be found in <u>The Family Blessing Guidebook</u> Chapter Five 'Why Look Back?'

140   Genesis 1:28

of secular humanism he would face? One of the answers was to find a way to *still do life together*. As I mentioned in a previous chapter, our eldest son David is a sports fan. When he was away from home attending university, we decided to do summer road trips together to visit Major League Baseball stadiums in the United States. Over the course of four years we visited almost every ballpark within five hundred miles of our home, from Kansas City to Boston's famous Fenway Park. We spent many long hours on the road together. Discussions ranged from the trivial to the purposeful. And whenever the truly important questions about life direction surfaced, we had plenty of time to talk them all through. God was at work and our partnership in faith has never waned since.

The principle of doing life together works for families at every age and stage. Here are some suggestions to prime the pump.

- Involve your children in the activities that are important to you as often as you can.

- Take your children to church and let them see you freely worshipping God with your upraised arms.

- Go feed the homeless together on a Saturday afternoon.

- Have a jar on the kitchen counter where everyone throws in their loose change for a cause you have chosen together.

- Get a report from that organization about the impact of your donation.

- Go find a place with a great view and sit there and talk about the meaning of life. Let them ask any question.

- Have some meals together where cell phones are banned from the table.

- Pray together.

- Go on mission trips together.

- Add a humanitarian activity to your next vacation and talk about what you are seeing and learning as you travel together.

One more thing. Do not pretend to be something you are not. Remember, the things we are pretending to be aren't transferable, only what we truly are. Part of doing life together is to still do it when it doesn't feel great. My personality type and character flaws were definitely the cause for some family arguments from time to time. One day I asked our kids about how my behavior had affected them. My youngest son replied, "What I remember most is that you were always quick to apologize." That really spoke to me. The thing that had made the biggest impression in the midst of my failings had little to do with why I was failing. Rather *it was how I handled that failure*. My apology became a teachable moment for all of us. That's also part of 'doing life together.'

> ## The things we are pretending to be aren't transferable, only what we truly are.

Picturing Your Story

"Tie them as Symbols…" Symbols represent visual learning. They provide a visual picture of the truth they represent. Symbols help us to remember. The Old Testament Law was full of symbols. In fact the entire Tabernacle, and all its myriad of details, is a visual picture of realities in Heaven. The feasts and ceremonies of Jewish culture include many visual reminders of the truths to be carried forward across generations. It works really well. As Christians we have the primary visual symbols of the cross and the elements of communion. The night before Jesus was crucified, He held up *symbols* of his body and blood for His disciples to see so that they would *remember His death*. Two thousand years later we are still impacted during a communion service when we hold the little cup of juice and the small piece of bread (or gluten-free cracker).

What does visual learning look like in your home? It may start with displaying scriptures and sayings that represent your values, but it certainly doesn't end there. Moving beyond that, you can discover the power of ceremonies in the form of family traditions. They do not have to be elaborate to be memorable. Special occasion gifts can convey a cherished message as well.

<u>Rediscover the power of the Sabbath</u>

If you want to learn from the pros, have a look at how Jewish people conduct their weekly Sabbath.[141] For twenty-four hours each week, beginning at sundown on Friday, observant Jewish families rehearse the faithfulness of God and their own family 'God story' through a combination of ceremony, informal sharing and verbal blessings from the parents. It is a day filled with meaningful symbols, songs, foods and prayers that has often been the lifeline for Abraham's family during periods of homelessness and persecution. Despite all the times in history that Abraham's descendants have been persecuted or prohibited from practising their faith, Sabbath-keeping remains at the center of Jewish culture and the root of their unstoppable blessing.

Melissa and I engaged in Sabbath-style weekly celebrations with another family for a period of time when our children were small. We know from experience that it's a difficult practice to keep up in the midst of today's sound-bite, hurry-up culture. If you are going to give it a try, don't be legalistic about it, just fit the concept to suit your particular situation. Create some semi-regular traditions, however small, that provide a memorable picture of your family life. Special places, outings, meals together, especially in conjunction with holidays, birthdays and anniversaries will become pillars deeply set into the foundation of the story that travels to the generations that follow.

Recording Your Story

Do you remember Ethan the Ezrahite? Was he considered good-looking? Was he shy or did he talk too much? Do you know how wealthy he was, or what his house was like?

Neither do I. But I *did* read something he had to say recently. And so did you. It was the opening statement to this chapter.

> "I will sing of the Lord's great love forever. With my mouth I

---

141   A great place to start is the website aish.com

will make your faithfulness known through all generations"
Psalm 89:1

You see, Ethan was a composer of songs in the time of King David and Solomon. That's about all we know except that he was a wise man.[142] And that's all we *need to know* because none of that impacts our lives today. Yet his writings do. Ethan understood that *through the instrument of writing* he could transport the testimonies of God across countless generations. The very fact that I am sharing some of his words with you today proves him right. As they say, 'the pen is mightier than the sword'.

Writing can serve as a time capsule for future generations.

Ethan had only a quill and papyrus. It was sufficient for him to send a message of the faithfulness of God down the generational lines. Today we have multiple forms of media. Ironically these can be the very things that keep us from telling the message of God's faithfulness. We tend to load up Facebook pages, Instagram, Twitter and YouTube accounts with super-meaningful and enduring stuff like a picture of today's tasty dessert or a selfie from a cruise. Okay, I'm guilty of that too. It's fun and harmless. The problem arises when those things so clutter our minds that we do not take the time to also write about the God story that is happening around us.

It's motivating to think that writing can serve as a time capsule for future generations. Here's an example from a young friend of mine named Jake, a seventh generation Christian who has 'World Shaper' written all over him:

> "We are often taught to believe that between generations are gaps. We are almost programmed to believe that this division, and separation is to be expected. I believe we think this way because we don't understand other generations. We have not experienced the moments they have experienced. We don't share the formative moments from the previous generation, so

---

142   1 Kings 4:31

*we judge it. The Great Depression? Just a distant story. World wars? Not happening again anytime soon. President so and so? Before my time.... Generations, from my perspective are the veins that bring life. I say this because **I have had the incredible experience of being able to read things my great, great, great, great grandfather, wrote prior to his passing** on Prince Edward Island. What I realized at that moment was that there existed a tangible generational blessing in my family, a mantle so to speak, that led to much of the success I experience in my walk with Christ."*

Jake is feeling the impact in the twenty-first century of words written by a family member five generations before during the nineteenth century. That shouldn't surprise us. You are able to set aside the barriers of time when you write. *Insights have no 'best before' date.* You can place them into a time capsule and they will come out fresh every time. *Do* try this at home! You don't have to sound profound, just capture the 'God story' in the moment. One day someone will read it just when they need it.

There is *one more* important method for sending the blessing forward through generations and that would be prayers of faith. That's covered in the next chapter.

CHAPTER 16

Unstoppable Prayers

God isn't offended by your biggest dreams or boldest prayers.
He is offended by anything less.
Mark Batterson

Shortly after Melissa and I broke the news that we were having our third child within five years, some older members of our church felt they needed to break the news to *us* about the trouble we would face. Did we not realize that one day we would have *three teenagers* in our home at the same time? "Two teenagers at one time is bad enough!" they warned. I wasn't totally convinced they were right, however these prophets of doom did manage to sow seeds of doubt. Could I be deceiving myself by thinking everything was going to be OK?

Discovering the Prayer of Faith

Surprisingly, the matter became settled in my heart after listening to a single mother pray one remarkable prayer in faith. I cannot recall her name, but I can still hear her words. This spiritual watershed occurred during a prayer meeting on the topic of families. In the midst of some very polite 'churchy' prayers, a single mother stood to her feet and started to remind God of 'their' agreement for her family. Apparently not all her children were serving the Lord at that moment, yet no anxious words fell from her lips. She looked up, pointed her finger heavenward and declared with utter confidence:

> *"Father, I told you when they were born that I REFUSE to*
> *raise a child for the devil!"*

Next came a series of declarations of what she expected God to do on behalf of her family. I was captivated by the sense of finality and confidence in her prayers. Her words flowed from revelatory faith that the Heavenly Father was willing and able to lovingly intervene in the lives of the children she had brought into this world. This prayer warrior had long since settled the issue about where her children would spend eternity. At that moment, renewed faith sealed the issue in my heart. I recall saying to myself, "YES! *She's right.*

I do not have to wonder whether my children will serve God. I have the right to settle the issue in faith now." So I did. And since then I haven't wavered.

> When we allow our doubts
> and fears to inform the way
> we pray, we risk forfeiting
> the Spiritual authority
> available to us.

To this day, many of the prayers my wife, Melissa, and I pray for family members consist of agreement prayers with declarations of faith. Do I believe that my prayers override my children's freedom of choice in the matter? No, I don't. It *is* possible for an individual to resist the will of God. On the other hand, God always honors faith when it is based upon His revealed will. That apparent paradox will be resolved for us in Heaven. In the meantime, I truly believe that *our default position on these matters is that God will answer the prayer of faith.* When we allow our doubts and fears to inform the way we pray, we risk forfeiting the Spiritual authority available to us in that particular situation.

Boldness that Pleases God

There are different kinds of boldness. There is a kind of boldness, based upon ignorance of risk, which can produce behavior that is brash and foolish. As they say, 'fools go where angels fear to tread.' That's not what I mean. The kind of boldness that pleases God is based upon relationship. You see this in the parable of the man who wakes up his neighbour at midnight to ask for bread. Jesus *praised* that man's boldness.[143]

One of the most shamelessly audacious prayers you will ever come across can be found in Genesis 18:16-33. I hope that as we mull it over together that it will impact your prayer life as profoundly as it has mine. The chapter begins by saying that the Lord visited Abraham by sending 'three men'. According to scholars, the three men were likely two angels and one very important

---

143   Luke 11:5-8

high ranking angel, or perhaps the Lord Jesus himself[144]. After revealing to Abraham and Sarah that their long-awaited child would be born the following year, the Lord also reveals that He is about to enact a rare and serious judgment upon the cities of Sodom and Gomorrah[145]. As the other two men (later identified as angels[146]) head toward the city of Sodom, Abraham intervenes directly with the Lord in order to challenge His plans *and change His mind* on the matter. Let's pick up the story from there:

> 'The men turned away and went toward Sodom, but Abraham remained standing before the Lord.[147] Then Abraham approached him and said: "Will you sweep away the righteous with the wicked? What if there are fifty righteous people in the city? Will you really sweep it away and not spare the place for the sake of the fifty righteous people in it? Far be it from you to do such a thing—to kill the righteous with the wicked, treating the righteous and the wicked alike. Far be it from you! Will not the Judge of all the earth do right?"

> The Lord said, "If I find fifty righteous people in the city of Sodom, I will spare the whole place for their sake."

> Then Abraham spoke up again: "Now that I have been so bold as to speak to the Lord, though I am nothing but dust and ashes, what if the number of the righteous is five less than fifty? Will you destroy the whole city for lack of five people?"

---

144   A pre-incarnation appearance of Jesus in human form, i.e. *before* his birth on earth in Bethlehem, is called a Christophany. Many scholars believe this occurred more than once during the period of the Old Testament including in this passage.

145   The inhabitants of Sodom were judged for much more than sexual sin. Ezekiel 16:9 NIV says *'Now this was the sin of your sister Sodom: She and her daughters were arrogant, overfed and unconcerned; they did not help the poor and needy.'*

146   Genesis 19:1

147   See footnote 2

"If I find forty-five there," He said, "I will not destroy it."

Once again he spoke to Him, "What if only forty are found there?"

He said, "For the sake of forty, I will not do it."

Then he said, "May the Lord not be angry, but let me speak. What if only thirty can be found there?"

He answered, "I will not do it if I find thirty there."

Abraham said, "Now that I have been so bold as to speak to the Lord, what if only twenty can be found there?"

He said, "For the sake of twenty, I will not destroy it."

Then he said, "May the Lord not be angry, but let me speak just once more. What if only ten can be found there?"

He answered, "For the sake of ten, I will not destroy it."

When the Lord had finished speaking with Abraham, He left, and Abraham returned home."[148]

Picture this with me. Abraham is at the feet of this person whom the Bible calls 'the Lord'. With the angels already dispatched to bring judgment upon the city where his nephew lives, Abraham challenges the Lord saying "*Shall not the Judge of all the earth do right?*" In other words: "You can't do that, God! It will violate your own character!" Where did Abraham's extraordinary confidence originate from?

It was the fruit of revealed destiny. A destiny revealed by God's voice over the course of years past and also through the words spoken at that moment. Here are those words:

---

148   Genesis 18:22-33 NIV

> Then the Lord said, "Shall I hide from Abraham what I am about to do?... For I have chosen him, so that he will direct his children and his household after him to keep the way of the Lord by doing what is right and just, so that the Lord will bring about for Abraham what He has promised him."[149]

Abraham knew beyond a shadow of a doubt that he had been granted authority to direct his descendants' spiritual welfare. Consequently, Abraham prayed with unprecedented boldness. Essentially he was saying to God, "I have family in that city and they are covered under my family blessing. You cannot wipe out the city until you first remove each one of them out of harm's way!" And so we see the most curious Q & A conversation in the entire Bible. When the Lord starts with the number fifty, Abraham is determined to work him down to ten. Once the Lord says that judgment will be held back even for the sake of ten righteous persons residing in the city, Abraham is satisfied and ceases his demands. *Why ten?* My simple explanation is that the number of persons in nephew Lot's household, including children, spouses and servants, added up to *eleven*! Abraham reasoned that if the Lord would spare the city while ten righteous persons were inside the walls, then Lot and his family would be spared until they could leave. And that is exactly what happened. In spite of his lethargy, Lot and his family were dragged from the city and physically saved from destruction. Later, they made other bad choices and faced serious consequences. Yet that does not diminish the fact that Abraham's shameless audacity triggered the angelic intervention that rescued his family.

Setting New Limits

What is possible when just *one person* who understands their Spiritual authority refuses to buckle under pressure? Abraham's bold prayer set the limits of what was permitted and not permitted to happen to his extended family. That boldness was based on a friendship with God plus a rock-solid revelation of his Spiritual authority. Did Abraham really change God's mind on this matter? I think it's more accurate to say that God always involves people

---

149   *Genesis 18:17-18 NIV* The word used here for 'after' is Hebrew *ACHAR* meaning hind part or with respect to time 'afterwards'. Context for Gen 18 is Genesis 9:9 'Behold I establish my covenant with you and with your offspring afterwards" meaning not just immediate children but generational descendants.

in His plans - especially through their prayers. I believe that God's plan all along was to inform Abraham in advance of the plans for judgment, so that *he could pray a powerful prayer of intercession that would save his family.*

Abraham's bold prayer set the limits of what was permitted and not permitted.

Now put yourself in that picture. Are you aware that you also have the same kind of authority to influence the spiritual environment for your family? The New Testament scriptures support this kind of extreme boldness for followers of Jesus. I cannot find a single example in the Gospels where Jesus criticized someone for being too bold when praying. Jesus actually praises the man in the parable of waking up a neighbour at night for bread.[150] Jesus also praises a widow for her resolute boldness and perseverance for wearing out the judge with repeated requests.[151]

Abraham's boldness came from grasping the boundaries of God-given authority and praying to their very limits. What are *your* boundaries? The answer is often situational. We'd all love to have God meet us and bring along a couple of angels like He did for Abraham. It's doubtful that will happen (though you can always ask). Ask God to give you a clear understanding of your authority in the situation you are facing. He is pleased to grant you that insight. Once you know your authority, then you will know which battle to fight in prayer.

Some people are concerned about overstepping their God-given boundaries. I'm not one of them. Life has a way of bringing us back around when we overstep, as long as our hearts are teachable. I am far more concerned about followers of Jesus who live *way too far* inside the boundaries of His will. Your Spiritual authority was costly for Jesus to obtain. He paid for it with His life. Not using this costly gift is a tragic waste of His sacrifice. Remember, Jesus had some pretty harsh words for the guy who buried his talent instead of putting it to good use.[152]

---

150   Luke 11:5-8

151   Luke 18:1-8

152   Matthew 25:24-30

Conditioning the Atmosphere

The confidence I received from the Lord during that single mother's declaration prayer over her family has never left my spirit. I have cultivated that level of faith for my family and it has grown.

When our eldest son David enrolled in a secular university, with our blessing, a well-meaning friend was truly worried that I was being unwise. "*You'd better watch out,*" he warned, "*Your son is going to lose his faith in that environment!*" I have learned that fear often masquerades as discernment and when it does, it's a bad counselor. My wife and I rejected those fears outright for three reasons.

Firstly, we had long ago decided that "we refuse to raise a child for the devil".

Secondly, we had openly lived our faith in front of our children, and by the time each of them had graduated from secondary school, they had made a choice to 'own' this same faith for themselves.

Thirdly, the spiritual atmosphere in which my family lives is part of the domain which I have the right to rule.

And so we prayed from that place of authority to condition the spiritual atmosphere around our children even when they were absent from us. Our children's part in this deal was to make wise choices. For sure, my prayer life was a little more intense during the time our children were in college or university, but I never doubted that my 'sheep' would return to their fold, spiritually speaking. We had raised them to enjoy the goodness of God and to experience His favor. We were confident they would always come back to the green pastures God was providing for them. And they did.

I recall one moment in our son David's life when we needed to pull out all the stops with respect to exercising our Spiritual authority. As a teenager, David had a basic common sense and most of the time it guided him well. However, in his last year of high school, we felt that David had crossed the line by associating himself with a type of music that had totally unacceptable lyrics. Even though we banned some of these albums from our home, David had become a loyal fan to a Disc Jockey from Toronto whose radio program aired this banned music after midnight. Melissa and I decided that we would try to deal with this situation in prayer before confronting it in other ways. So we entered David's bedroom when he was absent, anointed it with oil and prayed the following prayer: *"We declare that the season of the pleasure of sin has come to an end now. We cut off all ungodly spiritual influence that is drawing our son into this behavior...."* We prayed more prayers of declaration, refuting the plans and access of the enemy in the lives of all members of our household. We didn't mention these prayers to our son. Two weeks later David looked a bit grumpy at the dinner table. He told us that for 'some unknown reason' that radio program had been canceled in spite of its apparent popularity. We tried to sound sympathetic but inside I was doing my happy dance. The cancellation of that show made it much easier for our son to separate himself from that kind of music and keep himself within the boundaries we set as parents. I will never forget how decisively circumstances changed in that instance when we as a couple exercised our God-given authority over the spiritual environment surrounding our family.

Parents, it is your part of your job description to set the spiritual atmosphere in which your family lives. It is your children's responsibility to choose righteous behavior. They are much more likely to do so when ungodly temptations are removed from their lives.

This principle applies in other facets of life as well. Understand your Spiritual authority in the area you have a need for God to intervene. Then pray bold prayers that extend to the boundaries of that authority!

> The prayer of faith does
> not work until the prayer of
> repentance has done its work.

Repentance as a Weapon of Warfare

Although Jesus lauded those who pray boldly, He also made it clear that without the willingness to give and receive forgiveness, our prayers will remain unanswered.[153] I have observed that if there is unconfessed sin or a

---

153   For some of Jesus' words on this topic see Matthew 6:14-15 and Mark 11:25. Also King David prayed *'If I had harbored sin in my heart, the Lord would not have listened.'* Psalm 66:18 NET

fracture in an important relationship, then the prayer of faith will merely bloody its knuckles on a locked door while the key of repentance hangs nearby on the wall. Another way of saying this is that *the prayer of faith does not work until the prayer of repentance has done its work.*

This Spiritual truth was revealed to me in a very direct manner. Shortly before the unusual prophet visited our church in 1995, another prophetically renowned person came to speak at a conference in Hamilton, Ontario. I had this strong sense that I would benefit by being prayed for by this man, though I wasn't sure why. I almost missed the conference due to my work schedule, but on the last day I broke free and unfortunately, so did my car. My beloved 1983 Dodge Diplomat had a personality quirk where it would begin to sputter and misfire as soon as a weather reporter called for rain. On this misty day, it stalled countless times en route to the meetings. Moving slower than a Methodist circuit rider on a horse, I made the 25 km trip in ninety minutes. The after-meeting prayer time was just wrapping up when I walked in. I hurried to the end of the prayer line and when the man of God laid his hand upon me, the Spirit of God immediately revealed two things about my life to him. The whole prayer time took less than ninety seconds but the two things he said were so important that I can still quote them today word for word. The one I will share here is '*Lord, I believe that You are giving gifts of repentance to Terry's church.*' That was it. Pure Holy Spirit revelation with no human additives. I had a lot of time to think about those words while I pushed my car home. I tucked them away in my heart and soon I would put them into practice.

Later that year, I participated in a national prayer conference. It was held the week before a vote was planned in the province of Quebec on whether or not Quebec would separate from the rest of Canada. If the YES (to separate) vote were to win, Canada would be divided into two pieces geographically with a separate nation in between. Who knows what consequences there would have been economically and socially? (Almost every Canadian out-side the Province of Quebec was against the idea.) Ten days before the vote, Gallup polls showed the YES vote was winning. At that moment in time, the division of Canada into two sovereign nations appeared to be inevitable. At that prayer meeting, around thirty of us entered into a public apology and act of repentance on behalf of issues relating to the poor treatment of French Canadians by English Canadians. Our apologies and prayers were inspired by the great Bible hero Daniel who repented on behalf of the sins of his fellow countrymen even though he himself had not committed those sins. We call this 'identificational repentance'. When our profound time of repentance and forgiveness was completed, I felt the Holy Spirit say '*It's enough. I have hundreds of others praying the same way across Canada this week and I have received the offering of repentance. Canada will be saved.*'

> When repentance has done
> its proper work, the enemy
> of our souls can no longer
> influence the outcome.

Just days before the vote, a hurriedly organized march to keep Quebec in Canada occurred on the streets of Montreal (our largest French-speaking city). At the very last hour, the tide of public opinion in Quebec unexpectedly turned and the NO vote won by the slimmest of margins (50.5% NO and 49.5% YES). Canada was saved.

Remember this: Repentance removes the devil's 'rights' to hinder our prayers.

When repentance has done its proper work, the enemy of our souls can no longer influence the outcome in the matter we are bringing to God. The prayers of righteous people who, like Daniel, repented *on behalf* of the sins of our nation, were a prerequisite to saving Canada from a disastrous event. Once the prayers of repentance had done their work, then the pent-up prayers of faith were free to do their work! Since then, I have seen other occasions when the marvelous combination of repentance and faith has given the devil a 'one-two' knockout punch.

Do Try this at Home
Your prayers are powerful too. Understand your authority in the matter which captures your heart. Remove the devil's influence by confessing any remaining sin regarding the matter. And then let loose with the most audaciously bold prayer you can ever imagine. In so doing, you will bring the Kingdom of God to earth and put a smile on the Heavenly Father's face.

CHAPTER 17

The 'Anchor Leg'

The most important part of the story is the ending.
No one reads a book to get to the middle.
Mystery writer Mickey Spillane

I've saved the best news for last, and it's found in the following scripture:

> *"Therefore we also, since we are surrounded by so great a cloud of witnesses, let us lay aside every weight, and the sin which so easily ensnares us, and let us run with endurance the race that is set before us, looking unto **Jesus, the author and finisher of our faith**, who for the joy that was set before Him, endured the cross, despising the shame, and has sat down at the right hand of the throne of God."* Hebrews 12:1-3 NKJV

This entire book has been devoted to 'running the race that is set before us'. Now, we will focus upon the One who serves as both the *Author* and the *Finisher* of your race. That would be Jesus. This truth is a game changer. It means your race is winnable no matter what situation you find yourself facing.

The Author

The word 'Author'[154] in the original Greek text can also be translated 'captain' or 'leader', but in this instance, scholars chose to use *author*. It has a very specific connotation - Jesus conceived this relay race of faith. He *authored* the original idea and wrote the plot line. He designed the course track, starting and finishing in Jerusalem. He solicited the team members. After waiting for 'ages and generations'[155] to begin the race, Jesus placed the Gospel baton into the hands of the original believers instructing them to wait at the starting line until they received the team jerseys (i.e. to be 'clothed' with Spiritual power, Luke 24:49). Jesus also served as the team trainer, using his brief

---

154   Greek *archēgos*

155   Ephesians 3:4-11 talks about the mystery of the Gospel being hidden for generations (v4) and ages (v9)

three-year ministry life as a sort of race preview complete with personal demonstrations and practice runs.[156]

Once He became fully obedient in life and in death, Jesus' work on earth was complete[157] *and it was time to prep for the big event.* Jesus used the few days between His resurrection and ascension to brief His followers on race essentials. He explained the Spiritual authority that he possessed (Matthew 28:18) and how He would share it with them. *This delegated authority would become the baton to be carried across the entire planet!*

Jesus then revealed the starting line to be Jerusalem. He instructed His team members to gather there and wait for the Holy Spirit to signify the race had begun. With this analogy in mind, Acts chapter one reads like the tension-filled moments leading up to the sound of the starter's pistol. First they assembled at the starting line…

Acts 1:4 "Stay in Jerusalem until…" **On Your Mark!**

Next we see them getting into the starting blocks of prayer…

Acts 1:14 "They all joined together constantly in prayer along with the women…" **Get Set!**

As they await with pent-up energy, anticipating an unfamiliar power, the Heavenly starter's pistol is fired …

Acts 2:2-4 "Suddenly, a sound like the blowing of a violent wind came from heaven…They saw what seemed to be tongues of fire…rest on each of them" **GO!**

Like runners exploding from the starting blocks, those who had been filled with Holy Spirit power began to preach the Gospel in multiple languages provided by the Spirit. Thousands came to faith in the Lord Jesus that day. This opening sprint on the day of Pentecost soon settled into a sustainable

---

156   See Matthew 10 for the sending of the twelve and Luke 10 for the sending of the Seventy-two.

157   Philippians 2:6-11

pace and the number of disciples kept increasing. Within a short period of time, successful baton passes were already occurring.

Two thousand years later, this race is still on!

Every day across this planet, thousands reach for that same Gospel baton. As they grasp it from the hands of people just like you and me, they are eternally forgiven, experience new life in the Holy Spirit and thus become qualified to carry the baton as well.

The Finisher

We also anticipate the moment that our final team member crosses the finish line.

Every championship team needs a finisher, a star athlete to run the fourth and final leg of the race, commonly referred to as the anchor leg. The final runner is said to be *running anchor*.

Our Jesus is the greatest
finisher of all time.

"Bullet" Bob Hayes ran anchor for the United States 4×100 metres relay team in the 1964 Olympics. A French rival, Jocelyn Delecour, remarked to the American lead-off runner Paul Drayton "You haven't got anything except Hayes", to which Drayton responded *"That's all we need, pal!"*[158] That statement proved to be 'no brag, just fact'. Receiving the baton in fifth place, Hayes appeared to have wings on his shoes as he pulled ahead of four runners and won the race.

Our Jesus is the greatest *finisher* of all time. The word 'finisher' in Hebrews 12:2 (NKJV) is often translated as 'perfecter', but in the context of the analogy in which it is being used, it makes more sense to use the word that indicates motion. The expanded meaning of the original Greek word is "to bring something to the end goal" or "to carry through to accomplishment".[159]

---

158   https://en.wikipedia.org/wiki/Anchor_leg retrieved April 2018

159   Vine's Expository Dictionary of New Testament Words

Regardless of how much or how little you feel you have accomplished with respect to your life calling, yours is not the final leg of the race. Whatever Jesus has called you to do, He will be there to pick up the baton and 'bring it home' when all the runners following you have done their part. Like "Bullet" Bob Hayes, it won't matter when and where He picks up the baton. Once it's in His hand, *every* team member that participated will receive a medal.

In the global sense, Jesus is running anchor for the entire event. Sooner or later, there will be a *final generation*. When Jesus physically returns to earth, somehow, in all His great power, whatever remains undone will be brought to full completion. I don't know how He will do it, but He will. Jesus will wrap up the entire race with the greatest finishing kick ever. No brag, just fact.

The Cloud of Witnesses
One last encouragement before we conclude.

> "...we are surrounded by such a great a cloud of witnesses…"

Who are these witnesses that Hebrews 12:1 says are surrounding us? Go back one chapter to Hebrews 11 and you will read about a few of them. That cloud is made up of countless heroes of the faith who have lived, suffered, conquered, died and are now part of the multitude worshiping around God's throne.

The significance of this picture was unexpectedly presented to me while riding my bicycle through some vineyards in the Niagara region. It was a beautifully warm and sunny day. As I crested a small rise, I was surrounded by vineyards and could smell the ripening grapes. The setting reminded me of the famous Tour De France cycling race. As I picked up speed on the downside of the hill, I began to daydream that I was in The Tour, ahead of the pack and pushing hard to stay in first place. My reverie was interrupted by the Holy Spirit's voice. In my mind I heard the words,

'There's a cloud of witnesses watching your life race. They have finished their laps and so they are depending upon you to keep it going'.

The image was so clear, and unexpected, that I was confident God was speaking to me. Once dropped into my mind, the idea began to expand. I realized that the Lord was exhorting me to be faithful for the sake of those who went before me. This cloud of witnesses were depending upon *my generation* to bring their efforts to fruition. If that was true, then perhaps one day I would also join that throng, eagerly waiting to witness how well the next generations would run their laps. What happened on that bicycle ride became the initial spark for this book.

Your Personal Finish Line

Let's give the last word to an actual track and field athlete:

> "*When you run a part of the relay and pass on the baton, there is no sense of unfinished business in your mind. There is just the sense of having done your part to the best of your ability. That is it.*"[160]

Don't worry about unfinished tasks. Just stay in the race. Remember yours is not the last lap. Your personal finish line will never be THE finish line. Your goal is to make *The Great Exchange*, a successful transfer of all that you have carried so that the next generation can use your *finish* line as their *starting* line.

Past generations are *depending on you* to make sure they did not run in vain.

Future generations are *waiting on you* with an outstretched arm for what you carry.

Keep Your Eyes on the Prize and pass the baton.

Then head for the medal podium, because Jesus will be running anchor for you.

---

160   Attributed to N. R. Narayana Murthy Accessed from https://www.brainyquote.com/topics/baton accessed April 2018

APPENDIX
The Power of Three in a Row

Here is a point form overview of the unique challenges faced by each generation based upon the life stories of Abraham, Isaac and Jacob as recorded in Genesis chapter 12 through 50.

These are provided here for quick reference and for use as a baseline for teaching this topic.

The Pioneer Generation: represented by Abraham

The Call:	To leave what's familiar and follow the voice Of God into unknown territory
Symbol:	The Altar
Battle:	Spiritual dominion - the right to rule
Main task:	Leaving the old to establish the new
The Price :	Loneliness, perseverance, living with unseen goals
The Prize:	New favor for the generations that follow

The Bridge Generation: represented by Isaac

The Call:	To stay within the inherited culture of God's favor
Symbol:	The Well
Battle:	The Battle of the Bridge - to remain calmly committed to the long term goal in the midst of an adversarial environment
Main task:	Secure both ends of the bridge - connecting the vision of the Pioneer generation to the generations that follow
The Price :	Separation from the surrounding negative influences
The Prize:	Supernatural provision with great increase for the next generation

The Occupier Generation: represented by Jacob

The Call:	To take personal ownership of the inheritance
Symbol:	The Tabernacle or Tent of Meeting
Battle:	Ownership of the inheritance by overcoming outstanding negative family patterns

Main task: Renewal of the original vision and adaptation to a new environment

The Price :   Overcome lingering negative family patterns and walk in greater purity

The Prize: Permanence! The joy of raising a world-shaping generation

About the Author

TERRY BONE

Terry is an Author, Life Coach and Leadership Consultant. He serves church leaders, business persons and missions workers by assisting them to make excellent life transitions. Terry worked as a software systems analyst before becoming an ordained minister.

During the years Terry and his wife Melissa served as Pastors of Lakemount Worship Centre in the Niagara region of Ontario, they led their church family through a time of renewal and rapid growth. During that period, they also raised their own family, which now consists of three grown *world shapers*, their spouses and seven grandchildren (so far).

Other books by Terry and Melissa include:

The Family Blessing Guidebook
Everything You Need to Know to have a Blessed Family

Luke's Ladies
Devotional thoughts from the lives of all the women in the Gospel of Luke and Book of Acts

More information at www.exchangezone.ca